CARROLL ROBERSON

The Christ

A Closer Look at the Events
in the Life of Christ

The Christ

CARROLL ROBERSON

New Leaf Press

First printing: February 2005
Third printing: February 2006

ISBN-13: 978-0-89221-610-9
ISBN-10: 0-89221-610-7
Library of Congress Control Number: 2004118187

Cover Concept by Left Coast Design, Portland, Oregon

All Scripture is KJV unless otherwise noted.

Illustrations on pages 33, 96, 189 by Stacie Walker

Printed in the United States of America

Please visit our website for other great titles:
www.newleafpress.net

For information regarding author interviews,
please contact the publicity department at (870) 438-5288.

DEDICATION

Without the power of Jesus Christ, who changed my life over 20 years ago, this book could not have been possible, for He gave me a new life, a new desire, and a place in His Kingdom.

Without the support of my lovely wife, Donna, I could not have spent the days, months, and years of study that it took to write this book.

May this book bring glory and honor to the precious Savior of the world. May someone, somewhere, read this book and see their need of Him!

Contents

INTRODUCTION

If one should travel the world searching through all of the countries and cultures and beliefs, he would find that all mankind, whether wealthy or humble, urban or rural, dwelling in a hut or in a high-rise, has a common need — the need to worship something greater than he is. Throughout the passing ages, man has tried to fill this void in his life by inventing gods to rule over the various activities of his life. Every religion in the world except one has this common denominator — that it was invented by man.

The one exception stands alone and is distinguished from all other religions because it is not a fabrication of man's lofty thoughts, but is a revealed religion. Christianity is the only religion in which the God who is worshiped *revealed* himself to man. Man did not create God or the idea of God, but quite the opposite — God created man. Because of sin, man became separated from God, and there had to be reconciliation between God and man. The bridge across that gulf of separation was provided by God when He sent a special person into the world that He created. This person was prophesied to the Hebrews of the Old Testament as the "Messiah."

"Messiah" comes from the Hebrew word *mashiach*, meaning "the anointed one," and refers to the *title* of the person. In the Greek language of the New Testament, the word for "messiah" is *christos*, translated into English as "Christ." When the Bible says, "Jesus Christ," it means "Jesus, the anointed one."

To learn and understand who this Messiah is we must travel back in time, before there were ecclesiastical organizations of the 20th century, before ministry turned into big business, before Charles

Spurgeon, before John Wesley, before John Calvin or Martin Luther. We must go back before Augustine, or the Catholic church, before the Jewish temple was destroyed in A.D. 70, and step into the early part of the first century. It was the coming of the Christ into the world that split the calendar, and changed human history. Although He is the Son of God and Savior of man, we will view Him here as Messiah, the Christ in human form, misunderstood and rejected by the Jews of the first century, offering the kingdom to Israel, during the troubled times when Rome ruled the world.

As we follow the life of Christ, we will see the Hebrew prophecies of old come to pass; we will see the historical, geographical, and political settings; and we will survey the spiritual application of the many events that happened during His lifetime. This book is filled with biblical truths, the meanings of Hebrew and Greek words, explanations of historical background, and faith lessons that are easily understood. Spiritual songs that the Lord has given me will, I trust, lift your spirits in worship to this wonderful person.

My aim is not to add to, or take away from the precious Savior of the world, but to present Him as He is. This is not a denominational work; this is intended to be for anyone who feels their need of Christ, and for those who want to learn more about Him. My aim is to better equip the saints for ministry, hopefully to encourage them, and to present vividly the Savior from both the Old and the New Testaments.

With the help of the Holy Spirit, I hope you will see, like countless Jews and Gentiles, that there is only one person who could have possibly been the long-awaited Messiah of the Old Testament, Jesus Christ of the New Testament.

So come along as we journey to the land of the Bible, and come to know the Christ, His miracles, His ministry, His mission.

The Land of the Messiah

The land of the Bible has been called many names: *Canaan, the Land of Milk and Honey, the Promised Land, the Holy Land, Israel*, and many more. This is one parcel of land that has a unique relationship with God. He even calls it "my land" in Jeremiah 2:7. God loves this land, and cares for this land. Listen to Deuteronomy 11:12, "A land which the Lord thy God careth for: the eyes of the Lord thy God are always upon it, from the beginning of the year even unto the end of the year."

It was this land where God called a man named Abram, for a specific plan and purpose. After Yahweh blessed Abram, his name was changed to AbraHam, signifying the breath of God had touched him. The land where God brought Abraham is the same region called Israel today. This little piece of land is the center of the world, and holds such an important place that nations have been fighting over it for thousands of years.

Israel is the hinge between three continents — Europe, Asia, and Africa. If one could control Israel in Bible times, they could control the important trade routes that connected the three continents.

The land of the Bible has a variety of scenery as well as a variety of climates and terrain. Even though Israel is only about 50 miles wide, and covers only about 8,000 square miles you will find mountains and plains, fertile fields and deserts, often just minutes apart.

In Israel there are seven species of produce that are considered to be a blessing from the Lord: *dates, pomegranates, olives, figs, grapes, wheat,* and *barley.* These symbols have been found on thousands of ancient coins and stone carvings throughout the land. Over 3,000 species of plant life and 450 species of birds are found in the land of Israel.

God promised to bless the people who blessed Israel, and to curse the people who cursed Israel, and this has stood true throughout the centuries. This land is called "the glory of all lands" (Ezek. 20:6). The word "glory" in Hebrew is *kabod,* which means "beauty and honor." This land is glorious because this is the place from which God promised to bless all the earth. This is the land where the Messiah, Yeshua Ha Mashiach, walked nearly two thousand years ago. This is the land where Jesus was born, lived for 33 years as a man, was crucified, buried, and rose again. It all happened here.

There is one place in Israel, the Dead Sea, that is the lowest point on planet Earth, 1,300 feet below sea level. It's interesting that God came to the lowest point on earth, in order to redeem mankind. This series is all about the man, Jesus of Nazareth, the Messiah, who has changed the course of human history. Just to think, it all started here

The Christ:

in the land of Israel, and two thousand years later, we have the wonderful privilege to walk on the very same land where the Savior of the world chose to walk. So since this land belongs to the Messiah, we will ask Him to take us by the hand, and walk with us through this Holy Land, and show us where it all took place.

Walk This Land with Me

In Song

God gave this land to the seed of Abraham
And for their sins He gave himself as a lamb.
Messiah came to set His people free,
Where He walked, His glory you can see.
Messiah, take my hand
And walk this land with me,
And walk this holy land with me.

Show me Bethlehem, Nazareth, Capernaum,
Samaria, Jericho, Jerusalem.
Messiah, take my hand
And walk this land with me,
And walk this holy land with me.

The mountains and hills of Galilee,
The place where You walked on the sea.
Messiah, take my hand
And walk this land with me,
And walk this holy land with me.

Messiah came to set His people free,
Where He walked, His glory you can see.
Messiah, take my hand
And walk this land with me,
And walk this holy land with me.

Written by Carroll Roberson. Copyright: Jesus Is Real Music (BMI)

THE ANNUNCIATION
OF THE MESSIAH

Luke 1   From the very beginning of the gospel
accounts, we see that the story of the Messiah is one of the supernatural. Even the birth of the forerunner, John the Baptist, was supernatural, with Elisabeth, his mother, being barren and of an old age. An
angel appeared unto the temple worker Zacharias, *Z'kharyah,* telling
him that Elisabeth, *Elisheva,* his wife, would have a child, and his
name would be called John. He would be a Nazarite, like Samson and
Samuel, and would come in the spirit of Elijah. So we can see that
even though the priesthood was corrupt, there was a godly remnant,
even in the temple in Jerusalem.

When we speak of angels, we are talking about the supernatural.
What happened in Nazareth, when the angel appeared unto the little
virgin girl named Mary, *Miryam, changed the course of human history.*
Mary, had never known a man before, but she was about to give birth
to the Messiah, Yeshua, through the power of the *Ruach Haqodesh,*
the Holy Ghost. We can see godly people in the temple, and in the
Galilean town of Nazareth. God has always had a witness, and He
always will have a witness.

No one in Jerusalem ever expected the Messiah to come the way
He did. God always does the supernatural in ordinary people and
places. And even though we have to acknowledge that Mary was a
very godly saint of God, we must remember that she had to have a
Savior as well. "And my spirit hath rejoiced in God *my Saviour*" (Luke
1:47). God was going to use this poor, young, virgin girl to bring the
Son of God into the world.

What did all of this mean? In the prophecy of Zacharias, we find
the answer: "Blessed be the Lord God of Israel; for he hath visited

and redeemed his people" (Luke 1:68). God not only was *watching* over His people, but now He was *visiting* his people. God was coming down from heaven and fulfilling the promise that He made to Abraham in Genesis 22:18. We can see that this was the beginning of a new era, the fulfillment of the Old Dispensation had come. May we never think that God is not at work in our world! He works in His time, and that time is certain to come!

THE BIRTH OF THE MESSIAH

1) THE HEBREW PROPHECIES

The first thing to determine is *when* was the Messiah supposed to come into the world? "But when the fullness of the time was come, God sent forth his Son, made of a woman, made under the law" (Gal. 4:4). So when the time was just right in the world the Savior would arrive. "The sceptre shall not depart from Judah, nor a lawgiver from between his feet, until Shiloh come" (Gen. 49:10). The word "Shiloh" means "peaceful," "tranquil," or "secure." The Messiah will be the one who brings true peace, and the sceptre will not depart Judah until he comes. The sceptre departed Judah in A.D. 70, when the Jewish people were scattered throughout the world. So this person must come before A.D. 70.

In the prophecies of Daniel 9:25, the Messiah will come 483 years from the time they start rebuilding the temple in Jerusalem after the Babylonian captivity. This puts the coming of the Messiah in the first part of the first century.

There were many rabbis who believed that the times of the early first century were birth pangs of the coming Messiah. Under Gentile oppression by the Romans, the Jewish people were being led by a corrupt religious establishment in Jerusalem who had joined hands with the Romans. The heavy taxation and the pagan worship of the Greco-Roman world had them surrounded. But there was a minority of the populace who was looking for the Messiah. Many scholars believe that the Messiah was born during the Jewish Feast of Tabernacles in the fall. We cannot be sure, but could this be why the apostle John wrote, "And the Word was made flesh, and dwelt [tabernacled] among us"? (John 1:14).

The earliest prophecy was in Genesis 3:15, "And I will put enmity between thee and the woman, and between thy seed and her seed; it shall bruise thy head, and thou shalt bruise his heel." As Galatians 4:4 said, He would be born of a woman. The age-old conflict between Satan and the Savior would be won by the Savior, the Messiah.

This verse also hints at the virgin birth with no human father, "the seed of the woman." Listen to Isaiah 7:14: "Behold, a virgin shall conceive, and bear a son, and shall call his name Immanuel." The word for virgin in that verse is *almah,* which means a virgin who is a young unmarried woman. Now this means that the woman was a virgin, unmarried, who would have a child without the help of a man. This prophecy was fulfilled in Matthew 1:18, "Now the birth of Jesus Christ was on this wise; when as his mother Mary was espoused to Joseph, before they came together, she was found with child of the Holy Ghost."

The Messiah would be from the seed of Abraham. "And in thy seed shall all the nations of the earth be blessed" (Gen. 22:18). This is fulfilled in Matthew 1:1, "The book of the generation of Jesus Christ, the son of David, the son of Abraham." The Messiah would come through the Hebrew race, He would be a Jew.

According to Genesis 21:12, He would be the seed of Isaac, and according to Numbers 24:17, He would be "a Star out of Jacob." Luke 3:34 says, ". . . which was the son of Jacob, which was the son of Isaac, which was the son of Abraham."

We know that He would come through the house of David. "Behold the days come, saith the LORD, that I will raise unto David a righteous Branch, and a King shall reign and prosper, and shall execute judgment and justice in the earth" (Jer. 23:5). David's father's name was Jesse, and in Isaiah 11:1 we find these words, "And there shall come forth a rod out of the stem of Jesse, and a Branch shall grow out of his roots." The house of David would be so humble and so lowly when the Messiah came that it would be just a stump, and the Messiah would shoot forth from that stump of Jesse. This certainly was fulfilled in Matthew 1:1, "the son of David," and in many verses in the gospels He would be called "the son of David."

Now, *where* was the child to be born? "But thou Bethlehem Ephratah, though thou be little among the thousands of Judah,

The Christ:

yet out of thee shall he come forth unto me that is to be ruler in Israel; whose goings forth have been from of old, from everlasting" (Mic. 5:2). This was fulfilled in MattHew 2:1, "Now when Jesus was born in Bethlehem of Judea." Many of the people knew that the Messiah was to come out of Bethlehem, the scribes said it in Matthew 2:5, and many people said it in John 7:42. It is only fitting that the name Bethlehem in Hebrew is *Beit-lechem,* which means, "house of bread," since the Messiah would be our "bread of life."

One of the greatest prophecies concerning the Messiah is Isaiah 9:6, "For unto us a child is born, unto us a son is given; and the government shall be upon his shoulder: and his name shall be called Wonderful, Counsellor, the mighty God, The everlasting Father, the Prince of Peace." In Hebrew, His name would be *"Pele, yo-etz, El-gibbor, avid-ad, sar shalom."*

The prophet Micah said that not only would He come out of Bethlehem, but He would be from eternity. This fits the verses in the New Testament concerning the Messiah in John 1:1–3, "In the beginning was the Word, and the Word was with God, and the Word was God. The same was in the beginning with God. All things were made by him; and without him was not any thing made that was made." And in Colossians 1:17, "And he is before all things, and by him all things consist." This is not to mention all the other prophecies such as: He would be a priest, He would be a judge, He would be called King, He would be called Lord, and He would be called "Immanuel, God with us," like Isaiah said.

2) THE HISTORICAL SITUATION

And it came to pass in those days, that there went out a decree from Caesar Augustus, that all the world should be taxed. (And this taxing was first made when Cyrenius was governor of Syria.) And all went to be taxed, every one into his own city. And Joseph also went up from Galilee, out of the city of Nazareth, into Judea, unto the city of David, which is called Bethlehem (because he was of the house and lineage of David): To be taxed with Mary his espoused wife, being great with child. And so it was, that, while they were there, the days were accomplished that she should be delivered. And she brought forth her firstborn son, and wrapped him in swaddling clothes, and laid him in a manger; because there was no room for them in the inn" (Luke 2:1–7).

Little did Caesar know that God was using him to fulfill the Hebrew Scriptures. The Messiah had to be born in Bethlehem and the taxation ordered forced Joseph and Mary to travel from Nazareth to Bethlehem. Jesus was born in a cave-like dwelling, where they kept the animals. It is commonly believed that Jesus was born sometime during the winter months between November and March, but we cannot be sure. I find it interesting that in Luke 2:8 the Scriptures reveal that there were "shepherds abiding in the field, keeping watch over their flock by night." In the old Hebrew Scriptures we find, "And thou, O tower of the flock, the strong hold of the daughter of Zion, unto thee shall it come, even the first dominion; the kingdom shall come to the daughter of Jerusalem" (Mic. 4:8). This is the same place where Jacob pitched his tent in Genesis 35:21, "the tower of Edar." The King of the kingdom would be born in the "tower of Edar" in Bethlehem. Lambs were never born in houses where people lived, and so the Messiah, the true "Lamb of God" would not be born in a house either, but in a grotto, or a cave, where the sheep were kept.

The announcement came to the humble shepherds, the lowliest occupation of that day. They would find the child lying in a manger — what was to be so significant about that? Well, a manger was a rock on the ground that had been hewn out for the feeding of the animals. In the words of Isaiah 1:3, Israel did not know who her master was. *The ox knew his master, the donkey knew his crib,* but Israel had forgotten the God who had nourished her. This Messiah would be an *obedient* servant, unlike the nation of Israel, this was the sign of the manger.

3) THE SPIRITUAL APPLICATION

God always does supernatural things in the most humble settings. In our modern-day world, we think we have to meet certain criteria before we can be used of God, but God needs nothing but a willing vessel, and a person to really trust Him. I believe this is one of the biggest problems facing the Church today. Our attention is on fine buildings, big ministries, and money. When Jesus came into this world, He chose to have none of these things. We have what we need in the eyes of the world, but we are missing the power of God. One of my favorite verses is 2 Corinthians 8:9, "For ye know the grace of our Lord Jesus Christ, that, though he was rich, yet for your sakes he became poor, that ye through his poverty might be rich." The Messiah's entire life would be marked by obscurity and humility.

The Presentation at the Temple

In the Book of Leviticus, chapter 12, we find that when a woman had a man child, after eight days the child was to be circumcised according to the Jewish law. So they brought Jesus to the temple in Jerusalem and He was circumcised. The Law said that after 33 days, they were to offer a sacrifice unto the Lord. A lamb if they had a lamb, and if they were too poor to have a lamb, they were to bring two turtle doves or two young pigeons. The Gospel of Luke, chapter 2, tells us that they brought the poorest sacrifice. But little did Mary know that this was a prefigure of things to come, and she had the "Lamb of God" in her arms, that would be offered up for the sins of the world.

It was the custom for the firstborn male child to be redeemed. This was called *pidyon haben,* where the priest was paid five silver coins for the child. Mary would have gone to the temple, washed herself in a *mikveh,* then entered the temple precincts, to the Court of the Women. A horn-shaped container was there, where she would have paid the sacrifice. It's interesting that five silver coins paid the Messiah's redemption, according to Jewish custom, but it was the blood of the Messiah, that would pay for the redemption of mankind. Later, the apostle Peter wrote, "Forasmuch as ye know that ye were not *redeemed* with corruptible things, as *silver* and *gold*, from your vain conversation received by tradition from your fathers; But with the precious *blood of Christ*, as of a lamb without blemish and without spot" (1 Pet. 1:18–19).

There was a remnant during those days that was looking for the long-awaited Messiah, and two of them were Simeon and Anna. Simeon took the baby Jesus in his arms and said, "For mine eyes have seen thy salvation, which thou hast prepared before the face of all people; a light to lighten the Gentiles, and the glory of thy people Israel" (Luke 2:30–32). Quoting from Psalm 42:10, Simeon prophesied over the baby Jesus and told Mary that a sword would pierce through her own soul also (Luke 2:35). Little did Mary know at this time what she would have to face in the future, as she would see her son die on a Roman cross.

THE VISIT OF THE WISE MEN

1) THE HEBREW PROPHECIES

The kings of Tarshish and of the isles shall bring presents; the kings of Sheba and Seba shall offer gifts. Yea, all kings shall fall down before him; all nations shall serve him" (Ps. 72:10–11). "All they from Sheba shall come; they shall bring gold and incense; and they shall shew forth the praises of the LORD" (Isa. 60:6). This was fulfilled in Matthew 2, when the wise men came from the east to worship the child Jesus. It is believed that the wise men had heard of the prophecies concerning this king that would be born from the influence of Daniel 600 years before. Daniel 2:48 says that Daniel was made ruler over all the wise men in Babylon. The teachings of Daniel were handed down through the generations when the Messiah was to be born. Archaeologists have found coins in what is now Iran, that prove the visit of the wise men to see the Christ child.

2) THE HISTORICAL SITUATION

Matthew 2:1–12 The wise men — we do not know how many there were — came from Arabia, following a star in the east, remembering the Messiah would be "a Star out of Jacob." They asked Herod the Great, who was the king in those days, "Where is he that is born king of the Jews?" King Herod was very troubled and he sent them to Bethlehem to search for the young child. Jesus was not a baby at this point; He was probably two years old by this time. The miraculous star followed them and stood over where the child was. They fell down and worshiped Him, and they presented unto Jesus gifts of gold, frankincense, and myrrh. They were warned by God in a dream not to return to wicked King Herod, so they departed into their own country another way. It is believed that one of the names of the wise men was Gaspar. For many centuries, scholars had thought that it was just a legend, until this century, when archaeologists were digging on the Iran-Afghan border and found some coins with King Gaspar's name and figure on them. Later, the foundations of his castle were found. Many believe this was one of the wise men who came to see Jesus.

3) THE SPIRITUAL APPLICATION

A person who is wise will fall down and worship the King of kings and Lord of lords. These wise men traveled for weeks and weeks to worship Jesus. Once we come to know who the Messiah really is, we will go to the utmost to give Him our very best. The reason so many do not worship Jesus Christ and do not live for Him is because they have never seen who He is and why He came into the world. And the Lord protected those wise men. God will watch over those who love the Messiah. Have you ever seen how wonderful He really is? Do you give Him your very best? One day, the Scriptures tell us, "That at the name of Jesus [Yeshua] every knee should bow, of things in heaven, and things in earth, and things under the earth; and that every tongue should confess that Jesus Christ [Yeshua Messiah] is Lord, to the glory of God the Father (Phil. 2:10–11).

THE FLIGHT INTO EGYPT

1) THE HEBREW PROPHECIES

W hen Israel was a child, then I loved him, and called my son out of Egypt" (Hos. 11:1). Many times in the old Hebrew Scriptures, Israel was referred to as "a son." The Messiah Jesus was to be the *greater* "son." Jesus was a type of Israel.

2) THE HISTORICAL SITUATION

Matthew 2:13–22 A fter the wise men departed, an angel appeared to Joseph in a dream, and told him to take the young child to Egypt, for King Herod would seek to kill the Messiah. So in the night they arose and took the child into Egypt. It is believed they stayed in Egypt for over a year. There are churches in Egypt this very day that mark the places where, legends say, Joseph and Mary and the Christ child lived. Places like Wadi Natroun and Mostorod have long been sacred places where many believe the young Christ child lived for a short while.

King Herod became very angry, as he often did, and he slew all the children two years old and under that were in Bethlehem, and the surrounding area. The Gospel of Matthew tells us that this fulfilled that which was spoken by Jeremiah the prophet (Jer. 31:15) saying, "In Rama was there a voice heard, lamentation, and weeping, and great mourning, Rachel weeping for her children, and would not be comforted, because they are not" (Matt. 2:18). In Genesis 30:1, Rachel, the wife of Jacob, was barren, and she was so grieved because she could not bare children. But after much weeping, God opened her womb, and she had a son named Joseph. Her weeping and mourning was heard when the women in Bethlehem wept for their children being killed by King Herod the Great.

After King Herod died, the angel appeared again unto Joseph, and told him to take Mary and the young child back to Israel, but when he heard that Archelaus, King Herod's son, reigned in Judea, he was warned in a dream to turn aside and go into the parts of Galilee.

3) THE SPIRITUAL APPLICATION

We should always remember that the world has people who love Jesus Christ, and the world has people who hate Jesus Christ, like King Herod. Satan had tried all through the Old Testament to stamp out the "seed of the woman." Here, Satan was working through King Herod trying to destroy the Messiah. Until the Messiah returns, there will always be evil people trying to destroy the work of the Lord. The world system is anti-God, and many who hold high positions in this world will try to undermine our faith in Christ. Sometimes it is the wicked people who prosper and have power (read Ps. 73) and sometimes it is the wicked people who have the greatest following. We should never be guilty of just looking at the crowds or what is the most popular. If Jesus the Messiah was attacked by Satan, how much more will we be attacked? The good news is that God will make a way of escape for His children. Just like He provided the means for Joseph and Mary to take Jesus into Egypt, with the supernatural and the natural (probably financed with the gifts of the wise men), He will provide a way for us as well. When great things are about to happen for God, Satan is lurking in the shadows.

Application

THE BOYHOOD
IN NAZARETH

We know very little about the boyhood of Jesus, but we are given a powerful verse in Luke 2:40, "And the child grew, and waxed strong in spirit, filled with wisdom: and the grace of God was upon him." We do know that Jesus spent most of His earthly life here, all but three or four years of His public ministry. It is very interesting that the prophet Isaiah said, "For he shall grow up before him as a tender plant, and as a root out of dry ground" (Isa. 53:2). This tells us that Jesus would have grown up with peasant parents, in a little obscure, despised, disregarded valley, and He would make himself of no reputation. No miracles would be performed during His childhood. Jesus would have been a part of the Jewish community, a Jewish family called *mishpachah*. They were taught how to contribute to their families and their communities, not the individualism we have in the Western culture. No doubt, the Messiah grew up in a very religious home, and was taught the Hebrew scriptures from a very early age. The gospels do not invent some big events during His childhood, which shows the accuracy of the Scriptures. But Matthew's gospel tells us that Jesus growing up in Nazareth was a fulfillment of the old Hebrew Scriptures, "He shall be called a Nazarene" (Matt. 2:23). This name, "Jesus of Nazareth," would go with Him all the days of His life. It would even be written on His cross. The early apostles would call Him "Jesus of Nazareth." In Hebrew, His name was *Yeshua min Notzri,* Jesus of Nazareth, or *Yeshua ben Yoseph,* Jesus, the son of Joseph.

The Hebrew word for Nazareth is *netzer,* and it means "branch," and this is believed to be what Matthew was talking about. "And there shall come forth a rod out of the stem of Jesse, and *a Branch* shall grow out of his roots" (Isa. 11:1). The Messiah would be "the Branch" by the prophets Jeremiah and Zechariah. Jesus of Nazareth, "the Branch" that would shoot forth out of a little village would change the course of the world. Great prophets like Jonah, Elijah, Hosea, and Nahum, were from Galilee, and now the Messiah would arise. Many of the people were wrong in John 7:52, when they said, "Search and look: for out of Galilee ariseth no prophet." If they had known the Scriptures better, they would have known who the Messiah was. Also, one of the major trade routes of the day went by Nazareth, and people from all over the known world were traveling by the hometown of Jesus. This was a symbol that this child who grew up in Nazareth had come for not just the Jews, but for *all* people.

Jesus in the Temple

Luke 2:41–50   We know that Jesus was raised in a religious family because they attended the Jewish feasts each year. It was not mandatory that the women go, but here we find Mary with Joseph and Jesus at the Feast of Passover in Jerusalem. After the feast, they were on their journey back to Nazareth, but Jesus stayed behind. They thought He was with them, but after a day's journey they could not find Him among the relatives. They searched for three days until they found Jesus in the temple, hearing the religious leaders, and also asking them questions, which was the Jewish way of discussion in those days. After Mary spoke up and said they had been through much worry looking for Him, Jesus said something very powerful, "How is it that ye sought me? Wist ye not that I must be about my Father's business?"

By the time a Jewish boy reached the age of 12, he was called *ben hat-torah,* or "son of the law." This was the turning point of manhood, and even at the age of 12, Jesus was astonishing the people with His knowledge of the Word. There is no way we can understand in our culture the importance of the Holy Scriptures, as they were in the time of Jesus. If we would start teaching our children the Scriptures at the age of five, what a difference it would make in their lives and the lives of others. Why should we be surprised that Yeshua knew the Scriptures at such an early age? After all, He was the "Word."

In the time of Jesus, there were four major groups of people. There were the *Sadducees*, the *Pharisees*, the *Essenes*, and the *Nationalists* (Zealots). The Sadducees had joined hands with the Romans, and the temple leaders were corrupt hirelings. They were the wealthy aristocrats of the day. It was all about money and position. The Pharisees were supposedly the spiritual people of the day, who controlled the synagogues, but they had become hypocrites, "blind leaders of the blind." After the exile, when Israel returned to the land, local synagogues were established all over Israel. But they were following the "oral law," man-made traditions, along with the written law of God. That's why you can always hear Jesus in the gospels correcting them, saying, "Ye have heard that it was said." The modern-day church is also following man-made traditions, and in many cases does not even know the true meaning of the Scriptures. I wonder what Jesus would say to us?

The Essenes saw the hypocrisy of the temple leaders, and they secluded themselves into an ascetic lifestyle down at the Dead Sea. They believed in isolating oneself from the world, and ritual washings daily. They were the ones who wrote the Dead Sea scrolls, and were destroyed by the Romans in A.D. 66. (Some scholars believe that John the Baptist was a member of the Essenes.)

The Zealots hid out in the mountains of Galilee, refusing to pay taxes to the Romans. This also made it more difficult for Jesus, because the religious leaders thought He was just another trouble-maker from Galilee. The Zealots were willing to fight for their independence, and this is what they wanted Jesus to do — lead a revolt against the Romans.

But the majority of the populace did not belong to either of the groups. They were just common people of the land. This is what Jesus was, a man of the people. When He came to Jerusalem, no doubt His heart was thrilled when He saw the beautiful gold and white marble temple from the Mount of Olives. But when He went in and heard what the leaders were saying, it troubled Him. The real work of the Kingdom would come to the common people, not to the religious groups of the day, and may I add, that is still the way it is today in our world. So we can see Jesus here already setting the mood for what was to come throughout His ministry. If the Messiah saw through the religious system at the age of 12, how much more would He see later on? The religious establishment would turn against Jesus, always trying to trap Him, and eventually would take a major part, historically, in crucifying the son of God.

A Carpenter's Son in Nazareth

Jesus was probably not educated in the religious schools of His day, but rather at home. We know this from John 7:15: "How knoweth this man letters, having never learned?" Jesus grew up in a very humble setting. Nazareth was a small village, and Joseph would have made very little working as a carpenter in those days. It is possible that Joseph and Jesus may have worked in the nearby Roman city of Sepphoris, because it was under construction in the days of Jesus' childhood. We all need to remember that the Messiah living a simple life proves that we can easily miss the true meaning of life and get caught up in the modernistic, materialistic world.

We know that the Messiah spoke more than one language — Hebrew, Aramaic, and most likely, Greek. It was, and is, very common for people in Israel to speak multiple languages. (Our guide when we travel to the Holy Land, Dvora Maor, speaks five languages.) The culture in Jesus' time was very diverse, with the religious Jews and the Greco-Roman people living side by side.

It has been commonly thought in the Eastern world that Jesus was a worker with wood, and no doubt He was. But the word "carpenter," in Greek, is *tekton*, which means "a builder." All of the houses in those days were made of stone, so Jesus would have worked mostly as a mason, using stones, and also wood for the doors, plows, tables, etc. Jesus used the wooden farming implements in His teachings, such as, "Take my yoke upon you, and learn of Me," and "No man having put his hand to the plow and looking back, is fit for the kingdom of God." The simple life that He lived would help Him communicate His message to the common people. Things like flowers, children playing in the market place, and farmers in the field, He would use for backdrops to His sermons and parables. Many of the people in Nazareth rejected Yeshua as the Messiah because of His simple upbringing.

So the earthly life of the Messiah, growing up in Nazareth, would be one of working with His hands. One day, those precious hands would be nailed to a tree outside Jerusalem, for the sins of mankind.

THE BAPTISM OF THE MESSIAH

1) THE HEBREW PROPHECIES

The voice of him that crieth in the wilderness, Prepare ye the way of the LORD, make straight in the desert a highway for our God" (Isa. 40:3).

"Behold, I will send my messenger, and he shall prepare the way before me" (Mal. 3:1).

These were the prophecies concerning the forerunner, John the Baptist.

2) THE HISTORICAL SITUATION

Jesus was now 30 years of age, and His earthly ministry must begin. By now, a thunderbolt of a preacher, John the Baptist, was being heard down among the rocks, the serpents, and the desert: "Repent ye, for the kingdom of heaven is at hand." The fullness of time had come for the public appearance of the Messiah of Israel. There was great expectation during this time, because many saw the corrupt state of Israel, the falling away of morals, the callous hearts of the people. They saw the Roman oppression of darkness as a sign that something earth-shaking was about to happen. It was a time of transition, a time of doubt, a time of deep Messianic hopes.

John the Baptist never performed any miracles, and he never hesitated to say, "I am not the Christ." He was just a voice ushering in the Messiah. John was warning the hypocrites "to bring forth fruits worthy of repentance." Water baptism was a sign of identification in those days, and John's baptism was the baptism of repentance. So John was calling the people to turn from their sins and change their ways, because the Lord was coming.

John saw Jesus for the first time down at the river of Jordan. He said more than once, "And I knew him not." John and Jesus were cousins, but they never saw each other until the baptism that day. Jesus lived in Galilee, and John was from Judea.

When Jesus asked John to baptize Him, John said, "I have need to be baptized of thee and comest thou to me?" Then said Jesus, "Suffer it to be so now: for thus it becometh us to fulfil all

The Christ:

righteousness." Jesus went down into the water, and when He came up the heavens opened, and the Spirit of God descended upon Him like a dove, and there was a voice from heaven saying, "This is my beloved Son, in whom I am well pleased" (Matt. 3:14–17).

Now the question is, why did Jesus have to be baptized? He did not need to repent. He had never sinned! In the Old Testament the high priest had to be 30 years of age before he could start his ministry. He was washed, then anointed with olive oil. Jesus was now 30 years of age. He was washed, then anointed by the Holy Spirit, thus He would be our high priest. Also, Jesus was being identified with our sins, as man's representative, He was the God-man. When the Spirit of God descended upon Him like a dove, it was a symbol of sacrifice. The Messiah Yeshua would be the supreme sacrifice for the sins of the world. There is no wonder that John said, "Behold, the Lamb of God, which taketh away the sin of the world" (John 1:29).

3) THE SPIRITUAL APPLICATION

All who follow the Messiah must repent of their sins, and believe that Jesus of Nazareth is the Son of God. After we have accepted Him, then we follow the Lord's commandment, and we are biblically baptized. Baptism never was a means of salvation, but it is important, and every saved individual needs to be baptized. The scriptural way was by immersion, because it pictured the death, the burial, and the resurrection of the Messiah. Every time we take people to the Holy Land, there are always many who decide to be baptized in the Jordan River. There is no saving power in the waters of the Jordan, but many realize that they were never truly saved, or they want to rededicate their lives to Jesus. So if we are sincere about our commitment, we will want to be baptized. The question should not be, "Do you have to be baptized to be saved?" but the question should be, "What is to hinder me from being baptized?" like the Ethiopian eunuch asked Philip in Acts 8.

Down to the Jordan

I trusted Jesus as the Messiah
To take my sins away.
Now take me down to the Jordan River.
O, what a glorious day,
O, what a glorious day.

Down to the Jordan with me.
I'm not ashamed of my Lord.
Down at the Jordan you'll see
I'll never turn back anymore.
Now I belong to Messiah
And I want the world to see.
Down to the Jordan with me,
Down to the Jordan with me.

Written by Carroll Roberson. Copyright: Jesus Is Real Music (BMI)

THE TEMPTATION
OF THE MESSIAH

Luke 4:1–13   What a contrast! From the beautiful scene in the river of Jordan where Jesus was baptized, where the heavens opened, and the Spirit of God rested upon Him like a dove, to being driven into the desert to be tempted by Satan.

The King of the kingdom of heaven must face the prince of this world. "For this purpose the Son of God was manifested, that he might destroy the works of the devil" (1 John 3:8). The Light of the world had to defeat the power of darkness to prove that He was the true Messiah. Satan tempted Adam in the Garden of Eden and he fell into sin, and here the last Adam must defeat Satan. God became a man, and the human side of the Messiah must overcome the temptations that we all face in our lives. Also, Jesus was a type of Israel, who had crossed the waters of the Red Sea, and wandered for 40 years in the wilderness, then crossed over the Jordan River into the Promised Land. Jesus the Messiah came out of the waters of the Jordan River and went into the wilderness for 40 days to bring us into the Promised Land.

What was the temptation? Satan was trying to keep the Messiah from fulfilling His mission. Trying to keep Him away from the Cross where He would ultimately defeat what Satan had brought into the world. So what did Satan offer Jesus?

1) "If thou be the Son of God, command this stone that it be made bread" (Luke 4:3). Jesus had been fasting for 40 days, so Satan attacked the flesh. Satisfy the desires of the flesh Jesus. Jesus used what all of us must use if we too defeat Satan, the

written Word of God. "It is written, That man shall not live by bread alone, but by every word of God" (Luke 4:4).

2) Jesus was taken up to a very high mountain, and Satan showed Him the kingdoms of the world, and offered them to Jesus, if He would bow down and worship him. Here again Jesus used the Scriptures, "Thou shalt worship the Lord thy God, and him only shalt thou serve" (Luke 4:5–8).

3) Satan brought Jesus to the pinnacle of the temple in Jerusalem and challenged Him to fall down and let the angels catch Him before He hit the ground. The third time Jesus used the Scriptures, "Thou shalt not tempt the Lord thy God" (Luke 4:9–12).

This was not the last time that Satan would tempt Jesus. He departed from him only for a season, and he would return many times. So what does all this mean to us as believers today? Jesus was God and He was man. As a man He won the victory, and so can we if He lives within us. We are tempted every day of our lives to yield to the desires of the flesh, to have what this world has to offer, to show others what we can do in our pride. But the Messiah has given us the power to be overcomers. We are more than conquerors through Him that loved us. We must be filled with the knowledge of God's Word — that is the key. As long as we try to defeat Satan in our own strength we will lose every time. In Hebrew, Satan's name is *sawtawn*, which means "adversary," "false accuser," "arch-enemy of anything good." So always remember when we try to do something good for God, *sawtawn* will be around.

THE FIRST APOSTLES

Mark 1:16–20
Matthew 4:18–22
John 1:35–51

What a beautiful picture to think of Jesus walking along the shores of Galilee. As He was walking one day He saw Simon, or *Shimon*, and Andrew, casting their nets into the sea, and Jesus said unto them, "Come ye after me, and I will make you to become fishers of men." Immediately they left their nets and followed Jesus. Jesus walked a little farther, and saw two brothers, James and John, *Ya-akov* and *Yochanan*, mending their nets. He called them, and they left their father, Zebedee, or *Zavdai*, in the ship with the other hired servants, and went after Jesus. Now there had to be something mighty powerful in the call of these men to make them leave everything at once. Fishing wasn't just a hobby for these men, it was their way of existing.

Little did these men know what the next three years or so would do to change their lives and to change the course of human history. Jesus saw through all their weaknesses and strengths, and saw what they could become for the kingdom of God. They would make many foolish mistakes, but through their doubts, fears, and failures, Jesus would certainly make them great fishers of men.

When one followed a rabbi during the time of Jesus, they would walk behind the rabbi, and the very dust from his feet would enshroud them. They would learn from the rabbi, and it was the rabbi's responsibility to take care of them. They were called the *talmid*, or the *talmidim* if it were more than one.

One of the great chapters in the gospels is the first chapter of the Gospel of John. We see two other disciples named Philip and

Nathanael, or *Natan'el*. (Andrew and Philip were Greek names.) Philip found Nathanael and said, "We have found him, of whom Moses in the law, and the prophets, did write, Jesus of Nazareth, the son of Joseph" (John 1:45). Not one of the members of the scribe's family, not a son of one of the rabbis, not a man from Jerusalem, but "Jesus of Nazareth, the son of Joseph." Nazareth was a place of bad reputation, and immediately Nathanael said, "Can there any good thing come out of Nazareth?" When Jesus saw Nathanael coming he said, "Behold an Israelite indeed, in whom is no guile!" Jesus saw there was nothing false about Nathanael, he was the real deal. "Nathanael saith unto him, Whence knowest thou me? Jesus answered and said unto him, Before that Philip called thee, and when thou wast under the fig tree, I saw thee." In those days, the best place to be while meditating on the Lord, or studying the Scriptures, was under a *fig tree*. Nathanael replied, "Rabbi, thou art the Son of God; thou art the King of Israel." We have an idea about what Nathanael was studying about under that fig tree. Because Jesus told him that he would see angels ascending and descending on the Son of man, Nathanael was likely thinking about their great ancestor Jacob, and the dream that he had at Bethel about the ladder that joined heaven and earth, and the angels were ascending and descending on the ladder (Gen. 28). Jesus the Messiah was telling him that He was the fulfillment of that dream that Jacob had. Jesus was gradually unfolding the old Hebrew Scriptures to His disciples.

So these disciples would travel with Jesus, and be His closest friends. This call forever changed their lives.

THE FIRST MIRACLE

John 2:1–12   If the gospel accounts had been fiction, they certainly would not have put the Son of God being baptized in the river Jordan, by a man who was as ascetic as John the Baptist, then put Him at a marriage when His ministry started. But Jesus was the "Son of man," and we can see His humanity here as Jesus was invited to a marriage at Cana of Galilee.

The location of the biblical Cana is probably the Khirbet Kana, nine miles north of Nazareth, instead of the modern-day Cana. The original spot has never been excavated by archaeologists.

John, the writer of the Gospel, tells us that the marriage was on the third day of the week. The Jews performed marriages on the third day because in the Book of Genesis, when God created everything, it was only on the third day that twice he said, "God said that it was good."

It was a cultural disgrace to run out of wine at a marriage feast. So Jesus told them to fill the six waterpots of stone that normally were used for purifying, each holding 20 or 30 gallons. Then Jesus said to draw out and give some to the governor of the feast. The governor said, "Every man at the beginning doth set forth good wine; and when men have well drunk, then that which is worse; but thou hast kept the good wine until now." There have been many arguments over the years about whether the wine was just grape juice, or if it was fermented wine. Well, I do not want to argue with anyone, but as I have studied the Hebrew and Greek text, I have to say that it was real wine. The Hebrew word for grape juice is *aciyc,* "aw-sees." The Hebrew word for wine is, *yahyin.* The Greek word used in the text of

John for wine is *oinos*, which means fermented wine. Some people get offended because they have been taught all their life that Jesus would never have turned the water into real wine. But what people fail to realize is that Jesus was a Jew, living in a Jewish culture where wine was very common, and this was before the days of refrigerators or electric coolers. There's no sin in the wine, it's the drunkenness that is sinful. Jesus was accused of being a "winebibber," and the parable He gave about new wine in old bottles was certainly talking about fermented wine (Mark 2: 22). Jesus was not a drunkard, but He lived in the first century, when wine was very common (look at verse 10).

But people who want to argue about the wine are missing the main points about this beautiful miracle. Here they are:

1) This was the first miracle Jesus performed.

2) It manifested His glory.

3) The disciples believed on Him.

4) The old Jewish purifying rituals would be fulfilled in the Messiah's power to change lives.

John baptized with water, Jesus would baptize with fire. The law was by Moses, but grace and truth came by Jesus Christ.

Jesus was showing that He had the power to create out of nothing (Gen. 1:1; Isa. 43:7) — no grapes, no sunshine, no process of time was needed, just the faith to do what Jesus said, like His mother Mary said, "Whatsoever he saith unto you, do it." Through the work of the cross, the resurrection of the Messiah Jesus, God wants to create a new person within us (2 Cor. 5:17). It's not in rituals or baptisms or church membership, it's in the person who turned the water into wine at Cana. The Lord wants to do a new thing in the life of His church — 80 percent of the people who attend church are in a routine and they do not have the power of the Holy Spirit. Look unto Jesus the Christ, He will change you today, like He changed the water into wine.

THE CLEANSING OF THE TEMPLE

Prophecy

1) THE HEBREW PROPHECIES

Behold, I will send my messenger, and he shall prepare the way before me; and the Lord, whom ye seek, shall suddenly come into his temple, even the messenger of the covenant, whom ye delight in; behold, he shall come, saith the Lord of hosts" (Mal. 3:1).

"For the zeal of thine house hath eaten me up" (Ps. 69:9).

"For mine house shall be called an house of prayer for all people" (Isa. 56:7).

History

2) THE HISTORICAL SITUATION

John 2:13–25 Thousands and thousands of people each year gathered in Jerusalem for the Feast of Passover. They were coming from all the surrounding nations bringing Tyrian coins, Syrian, Egyptian, Grecian, and Roman. So there was a need for the "money changers." However, the high priest Caiaphas and his father-in-law, Annas, were so corrupt they were making a huge profit on the common people who were coming from far away when they exchanged their money. They were in control of the temple money. Also, they were jumping up the prices of the sacrificial animals — the lambs, pigeons, and doves — to an astronomical figure. So they were making money on what was supposed to be holy, taking advantage of the common people.

So just like the prophet Malachi had said, the Messiah came suddenly into the temple. This was at the beginning of His ministry. He made a whip of cords and drove out the money changers. "Make not my father's house an house of merchandise," were His words. The disciples remembered the prophecies, "The zeal of thine house hath eaten me up," from the Psalms. The Jews wanted to know what sign Jesus could show them as to why He cleansed the temple. Jesus answered and said, "Destroy this temple, and in three days I will raise it up." They thought He was talking about the building, which they had been working on for 46 years. But Jesus the Messiah was talking about His body. The disciples did not understand either, but after Jesus died on the Cross and rose again, then they remembered what Jesus had said in the temple.

3) THE SPIRITUAL APPLICATION

What a warning, especially to the church leaders in our world, and everyone who is in some kind of ministry. Don't ever make the Lord's work a thing of merchandise! There is a great disease in our churches today, of preachers twisting the Bible around in order to get rich in the name of Jesus. We should never take holy things and use them for our own self-gain. What would Jesus do today, if He were to walk into the average church?

JESUS AND NICODEMUS

John 3:1–21 It would be difficult to choose the most important chapter in God's Holy Word, but the third chapter of John would have to rate near the top of the list. This chapter has been misunderstood by many, so let's go back to the situation, the customs, and the meaning behind what the Messiah said that night to *Nakdi-mon*.

After Jesus cleansed the temple the leaders were furious, but there was curiosity in the heart of this man Nicodemus, who was a member of the Pharisees, or *P'rushim*, and part of the Sanhedrin. He carefully came to Jesus at night, seeing many of the miracles that Jesus had performed. He told Jesus that God had to be with Him for Him to perform those miracles. But Jesus, knowing what was in his heart, changed the subject and said, "Verily, verily, I say unto thee, Except a man be born again, he cannot see the kingdom of God, Verily, verily, I say unto thee, Except a man be born of water and of the Spirit, he cannot enter into the kingdom of God" (verses 3 and 5). Nicodemus had heard that terminology before, but not in that sense. For when a man was born of the seed of Abraham during the time of Jesus, he was pronounced "born of water" or " born of the flesh," a Jew. Nicodemus thought that being born a Jew made him a part of the kingdom. But Jesus the Messiah is telling him that being a religious man is not enough, he must have a birth from above, or "born again." This was so radical for this very good, religious Jew to hear. The wind was most likely blowing through the streets of Jerusalem that night, and Jesus used the wind as the perfect illustration. "The wind bloweth where it listeth, and thou hearest the sound thereof, but canst not tell whence it cometh, and whither it goeth; so is every one that is born of the Spirit." Nicodemus gave an answer that is very rational, "How can these things be?" The spiritual birth from above is past understanding, it is a supernatural working of God in a person's life. It's like the wind — you can't see it, but you can feel it. You cannot tell where it came from or where it is going, but you know that it is blowing.

Nicodemus had been pronounced "born again" on many occasions in his religious Jewish life. When he was 12, at his "bar mitzvah," he was "born again." When he was married, he was "born again," or starting all over. When he became a rabbi at the age of 30, he was "born again." When he became a member of the Sanhedrin, he was pronounced "born again." So the Messiah is using terms Nicodemus had heard before, to bring him to salvation. Jesus went on to tell him some heavenly truths that he had never heard before. The cross was very offensive to the Jewish people, but Jesus said, "As Moses lifted up the serpent in the wilderness, even so must the Son of man be lifted up." His death on the cross would make the born-again experience possible. And for a religious leader who thought that the kingdom was only for the Jews, Jesus the Son of God said these words that forever changed Nicodemus's life, and the lives of millions, "For God so loved the world, that he gave his only begotten Son, that whosoever believeth in him should not perish, but have everlasting life. For God sent not his Son into the world to condemn the world; but that the world through Him might be saved"(John 3:16–17).

And we know by the Scriptures in John 7 and John 19 that Nicodemus became a follower of the Messiah. He experienced that new birth that is like the wind. Every time I go outside and feel the wind blowing, I think about what Jesus said.

Jesus and the Samaritan Woman

Prophecy

1) THE HEBREW PROPHECIES

A bruised reed shall he not break, and the smoking flax shall he not quench" (Isa. 42:3). This prophecy concerning the Messiah says that the outcast people will not be thrown away. They used reeds for flutes, calling in the sheep, but when they became bruised they would simply break them and throw them away. The flax was a wick-like material that was woven from a purple flower that grows in Israel, called *Linum Usitatissimum*. This was used for wicks in the olive oil lamps. When the flax got down so low that it would no longer put out a light, they would quench it, and throw it away. The Messiah would take the bruised reeds, and the smoking flax of society, and use them in His kingdom.

History

2) THE HISTORICAL SITUATION

John 4:1–43 How grateful we are that the Holy Spirit inspired the apostle John to put the story of the Samaritan woman in the Bible. Because of the length of this beautiful story, I will try to be as brief as possible.

In the time of Jesus when the pilgrims left Judea, going back home to Galilee, they never went through Samaria, or *Shomron*.

The Jews hated the Samaritans, and the Samaritans hated the Jews. The Samaritans were half-breeds — half Jew and half Gentile. They believed that God was to be worshiped on Mt. Gerizim instead of the temple on Mt. Zion in Jerusalem. They were cursed in the temple at Jerusalem and their food was considered unclean, which shows how remarkable the whole situation is in John 4.

Jesus met Nicodemus where he was, a religious man who needed to know about the new birth. Here Jesus meets the Samaritan woman on common ground, He would use water as the metaphor.

Jesus asked her for a drink of water, and she noticed that He was a Jew, something that millions of professing Christians have never realized. She asked why He was asking her, a Samaritan, for a drink of water. Jesus answered her with one of the

The Christ:

great evangelistic verses of the Bible, "If thou knewest the gift of God, and who it is that saith to thee, give me to drink; thou wouldest have asked of him, and he would have given thee living water."

The woman, like Nicodemus, thought He was talking about physical things, so she started talking about the well being deep, and He had nothing to draw with. Jesus said, "Whosoever drinketh of this water shall thirst again; but whosoever drinketh of the water that I shall give him shall never thirst; but the water that I shall give him shall be in him a well of water springing up into everlasting life."

When the woman told Jesus to give her of this water, Jesus asked her to go call her husband, knowing what would be the answer. She said, "I have no husband," and Jesus told her that He knew about her five husbands and the man she was now living with. The woman changed the subject to religion, and said she believed He was a prophet. She started talking about where her father worshiped and where the Jews worshiped.

Then Jesus told her, "Woman, believe me, the hour cometh, when ye shall neither in this mountain, nor yet at Jerusalem, worship the father. Ye worship ye know not what: we know what we worship: for salvation is of the Jews." Jesus went on to tell her about the true worshipers who worshiped God in spirit and in truth.

The woman said, "I know that Messias cometh, which is called Christ; when he is come, he will tell us all things." Jesus saith unto her, "I that speak unto thee am he."

At this time the disciples came, and wondered why Jesus was talking to the Samaritan woman, but they didn't say anything. The woman dropped her water pot and ran back to the city, and told them that she had met the Messiah. Many of the Samaritans believed on Jesus as the Messiah, and He stayed in Samaria for two days.

3) THE SPIRITUAL APPLICATION

No matter how bad a person may be in our eyes, Jesus has a place for them if they will come to Him and drink of the living water. We need to beware of making the mistake of making people fit into our standards. It's good to have moral standards, but don't ever forget that a person may be nice, moral, and faithful to their church, and be outside of God's kingdom. Jesus said, "I am not come to call the righteous, but sinners to repentance. They that be whole need not a physician, but they that are sick." Sometimes we forget that the Messiah Jesus died for all of our mistakes, and He makes people righteous when they come to Him, no matter what has been in their past. Jesus was using this encounter to also teach the disciples, so when they went into all the world preaching the gospel, they would not have any prejudice toward other people. If a person had to be good, with no bad marks on their life before the Messiah would save them and use them, then we would not have the fourth chapter of the Gospel of John about the Samaritan woman.

THE SYNAGOGUE IN NAZARETH

Prophecy

1) THE HEBREW PROPHECIES

Isaiah 61:1–2   The Spirit of the Lord GOD is upon me; because the LORD hath anointed me to preach good tidings unto the meek; he hath sent me to bind up the broken-hearted, to proclaim liberty to the captives, and the opening of the prison to them that are bound; to proclaim the acceptable year of the LORD." Jesus read this prophecy in the synagogue in Nazareth. If you read the passage in Isaiah, you will see that Jesus did not read all of verse 2. The reason Jesus left off the second half of verse 2, is because it refers to His second coming, when He returns to earth.

History

2) THE HISTORICAL SITUATION

Luke 4:16–30   Synagogues were established during the years of Babylonian captivity, as meeting houses where the Jews could worship while they were away from Jerusalem. When they returned from captivity, they built synagogues all over the land of Israel. The ruins from hundreds have been found. There are three ruins in the Galilee area — in Capernaum, Gamla, and Chorazin. They were built out of the local stone, the black basalt rock of Galilee. You would have seen lintels over the doors with carvings of grapes, seven-branched candlesticks, vine leaves, a pot of manna, open flowers, etc. According to Jewish law, it took ten men to start a synagogue, thus making a congregation.

Jesus the Messiah came into His hometown of Nazareth and went into the synagogue on the Sabbath day, as was His custom. In the time of Jesus, they did not have the *Brit-hadasha*, or New Testament, they only had the Hebrew Scriptures we call the Old Testament. It was divided into three parts — the Torah, the Neviim, and the Ketuvim. This was the Law, the prophets, and the Psalms and historical writings. It was the custom to read a portion of each one, called "a string of pearls." Always, they would leave the people with a passage pertaining to the coming of the Messiah.

What is so amazing is that when it was time for Jesus to read His portion, they gave Him the Book of Isaiah, and Jesus opened the scroll to Isaiah 61:1–2, read the Scripture, then He closed the scroll, gave it to the minister, and sat down. All who were in the synagogue fastened their eyes upon Jesus, and Jesus said something that shook them to exceeding wrath. "This day, is this scripture fulfilled in your ears." They could not believe that the one who was the son of Joseph the carpenter would say that He was the Messiah that Isaiah prophesied about.

Jesus told them, "No prophet is accepted in his own country." He gave them the Old Testament examples of Elijah, or *Eliyahu*, being sent to just a Gentile widow in Sidon, during the three and half years of famine in Israel. And how Elisha, or *Eliseus,* was sent to only a Gentile leper named Na'aman from Syria.

What Jesus was saying was that the nation of Israel would reject their Messiah, and God would turn to the Gentiles. This made the Jews so mad that they took Jesus out to the brow of the hill, where Nazareth was built, and would have thrown Him off the hill, but Jesus passed through them. His hour had not yet come to be killed.

3) THE SPIRITUAL APPLICATION

Most of the time, the hardest people to witness to are the people in our own hometown. Jesus could do very little work in Nazareth because of their unbelief, and it will be the same with most of us. The most difficult area for me in which to minister has always been my hometown.

Also, this is a wonderful passage telling us Gentiles that we, too, can be healed of our broken hearts, we can be set free from our sins, if we will believe that Yeshua is the long-awaited Messiah. He was offering himself to His own people that day, and they rejected Him. He is offering himself to us today. What will be our response?

THE MIRACLES

1) THE HEBREW PROPHECIES

Then the eyes of the blind shall be opened, and the ears of the deaf shall be unstopped. Then shall the lame man leap as an hart, and the tongue of the dumb sing" (Isa. 35:5–6).

2) THE HISTORICAL SITUATION

And Jesus went about all the cities and villages, teaching in their synagogues, and preaching the gospel of the kingdom, and healing every sickness and every disease among the people" (Matt. 9:35).

Jesus performed miracles on people and nature, and cast out demons. The entire life of the Messiah was one of miracles. Beginning at His birth, Jesus was a phenomenon; the world had never seen anyone like Jesus. The people said things like, "We've never seen it on this fashion," or "We've seen strange things today." The disciples were astonished and said, "What manner of man is this, that even the wind and the sea obey him?" Of all the mysteries that we read about in the gospels, the greatest of all is the person of the Messiah himself. No wonder the apostle Paul later wrote, "Great is the mystery of godliness: God was manifest in the flesh, justified in the Spirit, seen of angels, preached unto the Gentiles, believed on in the world, received up into glory" (1 Tim. 3:16).

3) THE SPIRITUAL APPLICATION

The miracles had many meanings. They proved that Jesus of Nazareth was the long-awaited Messiah. They showed His compassion for people. The miracles of physical healing had a deep spiritual message. Jesus did not come to parade His miracles, but to set people free spiritually. Also, they showed all of us that in the future kingdom there will be no blind people, no crippled, no demon-possessed. It is a picture of all the ones who know Christ in the future.

How Jesus must have been moved to see all the sick and afflicted. He knew there would come a day when that would be all erased. Jesus walked among us. He knows the hurt and the sorrow we all feel. One of the things that touches you when you go to Israel is the *normality* of it all. He was God but He was man, and He lived as a man. He saw and felt what the common people were going through. Where the Great Physician walked, there had to be healing. Try to imagine how the word about Jesus spread by mouth by those people who were healed.

Long before the Bible was completed, the gospel spread first from the people who saw Jesus, and experienced His wonderful love and mercy. *Even though miracles still happen today*, physical healing does not have the same role as it did when the Messiah walked the earth. If some of these so-called "miracle preachers" had the power they claim to have, why don't they go into the hospitals and funeral homes, and raise the dead? The greatest miracle of all is when a person is changed by the power of God, when they are truly saved, and God's Spirit comes to live inside.

Over 30 miracles are recorded in the Gospels, but John said, "If they should be written every one, I suppose that even the world itself could not contain the books that should be written. Amen" (John 21:25).

MESSIAH AT BETHESDA'S POOL

John 5   It is impossible to trace the earthly ministry of the Messiah chronologically, but that is not the primary concern. We want to see the message that the Messiah gave, and see His person.

Jesus went to one of the religious Jewish feasts in Jerusalem; we are not told which one it was. While He was there, He noticed two totally different kinds of people: 1) The self-righteous, religious leaders, who had no true love for the common people. They were claiming to be godly people with their strict observance of things like the Sabbath Day. By the way, they did not even understand what was meant by the Sabbath Day. 2) Jesus saw the multitude of people lying around the pool of Bethesda who needed help, and were trusting in the wrong thing to get help.

The pool of Bethesda, *Beit Zata*, may mean "house of healing." We know that it had five porches, and was a very popular place. The people had a belief that they could be healed if they were the first ones to enter the pool after the bubbling of the water. The underground springs would cause a moving of the water at certain times, and the people had a tradition that it was an angel that moved the water.

Jesus heard the cry in the air of the impotent folk lying on pallets or rugs around the pool. The old Hebrew prophecies in Isaiah 35, said, "Then will the lame leap like a deer" (Isa. 35:6; NIV). Here is the fulfillment of that prophecy. Here is a man who had been crippled for 38 years, and Jesus came to him and asked him, "Wilt thou be made whole? The impotent man answered him, Sir, I have no man . . . to put me into the pool . . . another steppeth down before me. Jesus saith unto him, Rise, take up thy bed, and walk. And immediately the man was made whole, and took up his bed, and walked: and on the same day was the sabbath" (John 5:6–9).

The Jews began to persecute Jesus, and wanted to kill Him because He healed a man on the Sabbath day. Jesus told them that this was just what the Father sent Him into the world to do, give life to the dead people, and one day He would raise the dead in the resurrection. He gave them four witnesses to the truth of who He was:

1) John the Baptist — John 5: 33–35

2) His works — John 5:36

3) The Father — John 5:37–38

4) The Scriptures — John 5:39

If the religious people had known the Hebrew Scriptures better, they would have known who Jesus was. They thought they had eternal life, but they were lost. As we carefully search the Scriptures, we can know if we truly have everlasting life.

MESSIAH'S MINISTRY IN GALILEE

Prophecy

1) THE HEBREW PROPHECIES

Nevertheless the dimness shall not be such as was in her vexation, when at the first he lightly afflicted the land of Zebulun and the land of Naphtali, and afterward did more grievously afflict her by the way of the sea, beyond Jordan, in Galilee of the nations. The people that walked in darkness have seen a great light: they that dwell in the land of shadow of death, upon them hath the light shined" (Isa. 9:1–2).

Matthew says in Matthew 4:13–16, that the reason the Messiah came and dwelt in Galilee was so the Scriptures might be fulfilled.

History

2) THE HISTORICAL SITUATION

Now after that John was put in prison, Jesus came into Galilee, preaching the gospel of the kingdom of God" (Mark 1:14). "And Jesus went about all Galilee, teaching in their synagogues, and preaching the gospel of the kingdom, and healing all manner of sickness and all manner of disease among the people. And His fame went throughout all Syria: and they brought unto him all the sick people that were taken with divers diseases and torments, and those which were possessed with devils, and those which were lunatick and those that had the palsy; and he healed them. And there followed him great multitudes of people from Galilee, and from Decapolis, and from Jerusalem, and from Judea, and from beyond Jordan" (Matt. 4:23–25).

Galilee was a political and religious tenderbox, being surrounded by the Gentile, pagan worshipers. On the west was Tiberias, home of Herod Antipas. In the north was the territory of Herod Philip, and on the southeastern shore was the land of the Decapolis. It was also a place of political unrest, with the Zealots hiding out in the caves in the mountains, refusing to yield to the Romans. There were constant revolts led by these Nationalists (Acts 5:36–37). This made it very difficult for Jesus among the religious leaders, because He was from Galilee.

Jesus knew that He only had a small window of opportunity to travel and minister before His final death in Jerusalem. He started His ministry in the synagogues, then He would have to go into the homes, and travel from place to place. He would live among the common people on the northern shore. The farmers, the fishermen, the poor, and the outcasts would hear His message.

The land of Galilee, to me, is the most captivating place in the Holy Land. This is where the Messiah lived, performed those beautiful miracles, and taught those mysterious parables. It's my favorite biblical location, and we will spend a considerable amount of time here, as we reflect on the earthly ministry of the Messiah.

2) THE SPIRITUAL APPLICATION

Jesus spent most of His time around the country people, the *am-ha-aretz*. If you recall, Peter and John were accused by the religious people of being "unlearned and ignorant," in Acts 4:13. The lesson for us is that, God does *supernatural* things in *ordinary* people. The kingdom of God would be ushered in by the Messiah, to the poor, the blind, the lepers, the crippled, and the adulterous women. God chooses to take the child-like people to confound the wise. Jesus, being a peasant preacher, tells us that life does not consist of the finer things, but it is *within*. The Messiah made many poor people rich as He walked the hills of Galilee.

My favorite place in the world, is Galilee, and every year I can hardly wait until I can walk the roads where my Savior walked. Being raised by a common family in rural Mississippi, it moves me deeply to know that Jesus deliberately chose to live among the common people. I can almost imagine myself standing on the shore now, and here comes Jesus!

THE MIRACULOUS
CATCH

Luke 5:1–11   It had to be a source of refreshment
for Jesus the Messiah to be around the beautiful Sea of Galilee, away
from *most* of the religious hypocrites down in Jerusalem. What a
picture, Jesus the Son of God, standing on the shore with people
pressing upon Him to hear the Word of God. Jesus saw two empty
boats, and fishermen washing their nets from the sand and pebbles.
They were not allowed to fix any permanent nets in the sea because it
would hinder the busy traffic on the waters.

Here Jesus uses the boat of Simon Peter, *Shimon Kefa*, for a
pulpit, and teaches the people about the kingdom of God. When
He is finished, He tells Simon to launch out into the deep water
and let down the nets. Peter said, "Master, we have been fishing all
night and haven't caught a thing, nevertheless, whatever you say."
They would fish at night, so the fish would not see their fishing line,
which was made of cotton twine, not invisible nylon. Jesus tells
them to go fishing in the middle of the day, which is a poor time to
go fishing. But look what happened! They caught such a multitude
of fish that the net broke. They yelled at their partners to come and
help them and the fish filled both of their boats, so much that they
began to sink.

When Peter saw it, he fell down at the feet of Jesus and said, "Depart from me: for I am a sinful man, O Lord."

The disciples were astonished, and Jesus said unto Simon, "Fear
not, from henceforth, thou shalt catch men." The word in the original
text for "catch" is *zogreo*, and it means "to make alive." What Jesus was

saying was, when you catch fish, you kill them, but when you catch men, you will be making dead people come to life.

Jesus could see through the waters, and He knew where the fish were. Or maybe He just created that catch for the disciples. Who knows? But there is one thing for sure — when Jesus bids us to let down the net, there *will* be a great catch. There's not anything to worry about if we get our instructions from the Master of the sea.

After they saw this powerful miracle, they left everything and followed Jesus. There are three points of interest here:

1) It was a call for them to be persecuted by the Jewish authorities, for Jesus had already begun to experience it in Jerusalem.

2) It was a call for them to leave their earthly occupations, breaking ties with the world.

3) It was a call for them to become fishers of men, of which their former occupation was a symbol.

The Messiah is calling us as well, to be fishers of men. Once a person sees others through the eyes of Jesus, they can never see them the same again. Everyone we meet either knows Christ, or they do not know Christ. It matters not what their past may be, or what their occupation may be, our job as followers of the Messiah is to be a "fisher of men."

In Song

Cast Your Net upon the Sea

Cast your net upon the sea,
　　upon the sea, upon the sea.
Cast your net upon the sea
And see what God can do.

Jesus was preaching in Peter's boat one day.
When He was finished, they heard Jesus say

Cast your net upon the sea,
　　upon the sea, upon the sea.
Cast your net upon the sea
And see what God can do.

Peter said, "Dear Lord I've been fishing all the night.
How can we catch fish when the sun is bright?"
But nevertheless they cast their net
Like Jesus told them to.
Their eyes were filled with much surprise
They caught a multitude.

Cast your net upon the sea,
     upon the sea, upon the sea.
Cast your net upon the sea
And see what God can do.

Before Jesus left this earth He said at Galilee
Take the gospel to the world so others can believe,
And don't you be discouraged
Be faithful 'til the end.
Remember what I've told you
And where it all began.

Cast your net upon the sea,
     upon the sea, upon the sea.
Cast your net upon the sea
And see what God can do,
And see what God can do.

Written by Carroll Roberson. Copyright: Jesus Is Real Music (BMI)

A BUSY DAY IN CAPERNAUM

Matthew 8:5–17, 9:2–8
Mark 1:23–2:12
Luke 4:33–5:26

There are two things to remember about Capernaum, and the region around Galilee: 1) It was a place of darkness, and, 2) the Light of the World came here. The common people in Capernaum, were oppressed economically, religiously, and politically. The Jewish village people were trying to hack out a living in the farming fields or in the fishing industry. They were heavily taxed by the Romans, and were surrounded on the east and west by the pagan Greco-Roman culture. Have you ever noticed when you read the Gospel of Mark, for example, the number of sick people and demon-possessed people? It was a very dark time when the Messiah came into Galilee. But the Messiah came, and He brought light to many of the people there. In this section we shall look at a very busy day Jesus spent in Capernaum.

Here at Capernaum, *K' far-nachum*, the home of the earthly ministry of Jesus, there was a synagogue. The ruins are from the fourth century, but underneath it are the foundations of the original synagogue that may have been built by the centurion in Luke 7. While Jesus was preaching one day, a demon-possessed man cried out, saying, "Let us alone; what have we to do with thee, thou Jesus of Nazareth? art thou come to destroy us? I know thee who thou art, the Holy One of God." Jesus cast the demon out of the man, as a sign that He had come to destroy the works of the devil. The people were amazed at the authority of Jesus and His fame spread throughout all of Galilee (Mark 1:23–28).

The Christ:

When He left the synagogue, He went to the house of Simon Peter, where Peter's mother-in-law was sick with a fever. Jesus took her by the hand and lifted her up, and immediately the fever left her. She ministered unto Jesus, and no doubt became a sincere follower of the Messiah. When you travel to Capernaum today, you will see ruins from the time of Jesus. Archaeologists have found what they believe is the house of Simon Peter. Over the house was built a Byzantine church in about the fourth century, and now a Catholic church has been built over the site, but you can still see the ruins of Peter's house underneath. This is where our Lord healed Peter's mother-in-law (Mark 1:29–31).

When the sun was going down, all the streets of Capernaum were filled with sick people. He healed them all! What a sight! Can't you see hundreds of sick and diseased people gathering at the door of Peter's house, to see Yeshua? The *sun* had gone down, but the *Son* of God had risen (Mark 1:32–34).

Jesus would rise early before daybreak, and go up into the mountains of Galilee to pray, then He would travel throughout the towns and villages preaching about the kingdom of God in the local synagogues. The historian Josephus tells us that approximately two hundred towns were in the region during the time of Jesus. The mountains surrounding the Sea of Galilee have an unusual glory about them. I tell people who ask about our Holy Land tours that all of Israel is a witness of the power of the Lord God Almighty, but the scene at Galilee will make an everlasting impression on your life. Jesus the Messiah saw the same mountains that we can see today, and He walked across most of them. His prayers were uttered from these mountains, and *we* are the fruits of those prayers today (Mark 1:35–39).

In Mark 1:40–45, we have one of the "Messianic Miracles." Certain miracles that Jesus performed were, according partly to the prophet Isaiah (35:3–7) and partly to the old rabbis ("When the Messiah comes, He and only He will perform these things") sure proofs that He was the Messiah that the prophets wrote about. Miracles like healing a man born blind, casting demons out of a man who was deaf and dumb, raising the dead, healing the crippled and lame, and healing a Jewish leper.

The law concerning what a leper was to do if he or she were cleansed was written in the Torah, in Leviticus 13 and 14. But here is the mystery of it all — *no* Jewish leper had ever been cleansed. (Miriam had been healed of leprosy [Numbers 12], but her cleansing did not come through a person, but was from God himself. Naaman, in 2 Kings, was a Syrian, but his cleansing was not from the direct touch of a person, either.) So if no Jewish leper had been cleansed, then why put the law of the leper in the Torah? Because, the Messiah would fulfill that law, and He would cleanse the leper! Anyone was unclean when they touched a leper, but Jesus touched the leper and made him clean. Jesus told this man to go show thyself to the priest, just like the Law said, "for a testimony unto them." What mercy! Jesus was telling the unbelieving priests that the Messiah had come. The poor Jewish leper was so beside himself that he did exactly what Jesus told him *not* to do, he blazed his healing everywhere. This was a turning point in the Messiah's earthly ministry, for He could no longer enter the cities openly. He had to spend most of His time in deserted places, which also fulfilled Isaiah 35:1.

After some days, Jesus went back into Capernaum, and it was told that Jesus was in the house. People were standing outside the door to hear Jesus preach. Four men were carrying a man who had the palsy. They could not get in the house, so, they tore off the roof, and let the man down on a bed so Jesus could see him. In those days the roofs of the houses were flat, and made out of probably thatch or tiles. Jesus told the sick man something earth-shaking: "Thy sins be forgiven thee." Not only did Jesus heal the man physically, but He forgave him of his sins. This was blasphemy to the Jews, because the old Hebrew Scriptures said that only God could forgive sins. This showed that Jesus was not just a miracle worker, he was none other than God in the flesh. If we had been there that day, we would have said something like they did, "We never saw it on this fashion" (Mark 2:1–12).

THE CALL OF MATTHEW

Luke 5:27–39   As the Messiah was walking along the Sea of Galilee one day, He saw a publican, a tax collector named Matthew, *Mattityahu*. We need to try to put ourselves back in the days of the early first century, when the common people were taxed for almost everything. It was a time of great oppression and injustice. Taxes were placed upon all imports and exports — all that was bought and sold. Bridge-money, road-money, harbor-money, town-money. The Romans would even invent a tax, and find a name to justify it. There was a tax on axles, wheels, pack animals, highways, crossing rivers, and the ships that fishermen used, such as Peter and John. Matthew was not only a publican who collected taxes for the Romans, and kept part of the money for himself, but he was of the worst kind. He was the one "sitting at the receipt of custom," the one who collected taxes from the ships on the Sea of Galilee. To the Jewish leaders and the common people as well, Matthew was a man who could not be forgiven in their eyes. But the Messiah called this man, Matthew, to follow Him, and that powerful look on the face of Jesus made him give it all up and join the kingdom of God. It's interesting that Jesus would call a man that was so hated by the other disciples. Here, Jesus is teaching them the wonderful lesson of forgiveness. God can use anyone in His kingdom, no matter what they may seem to be in our eyes. It took the love of Jesus Christ to cause a man like Matthew to work alongside a man like Peter.

Matthew made Jesus a great feast in his house, and many other tax collectors came to the feast. In the time of Jesus, eating a meal with someone was a sign of forgiveness and reconciliation. But the religious leaders began to murmur against Jesus and the disciples, because they were eating with publicans and sinners. Jesus said, "They that are whole need not a physician, but they that are sick. I came not to call the righteous, but sinners to repentance." The scribes and Pharisees started condemning the disciples because they were not fasting, like the disciples of John the Baptist did. Then Jesus gave a tremendous parable: "No man putteth a piece of a new garment upon an old; if otherwise, then both the new maketh a rent, and the piece that was taken out of the new agreeth not with the old. And no man putteth new wine into old bottles; else the new wine will burst the bottles, and be spilled, and the bottles shall perish. But new wine must be put into new bottles; and both are preserved. No man also having drunk old wine straightway desireth new: for he saith, The old is better." What did this all mean?

The reason Jesus did not call the Pharisees to be His disciples, instead choosing mere fishermen and tax collectors, was because the Pharisees were trying to patch up their old religious system with things like fasting for a religious show. Jesus the Messiah, came offering a totally new system, the kingdom of God. He would start with new men and fill them with new wine, instead of trying to add His new teachings into the old Jewish system. The religious leaders desired the old traditions, and had rejected the Messiah's new movement. What a great lesson this is for all of us. We cannot try to patch up our lives with religious rituals and outward observances, such as fastings, long prayers, church attendance, tithing, etc. We must have a new heart, a new beginning — and that only comes through faith in the Messiah.

Matthew had found a new life, "forgiveness of his sins," *slee chat chah tah eem,* in Hebrew. When we realize that we, too, are sick spiritually, and need a physician, then Jesus will make us brand new.

Once again, we can see that God seems to do His greatest work of grace in the most unlikely places and people. The people of Galilee were in despair — here the Messiah came. Matthew was hated by the religious Jews, but it was to people like him that Jesus showed His great mercy and love. When we feel discouraged and downtrodden, this is a very good time for the Messiah to shine His great light!

THE SERMON ON
THE MOUNT

Matthew 5, 6, and 7   As we look at the synoptic Gospels of Matthew, Mark, and Luke, we find that Jesus had gone up into a mountain the previous night and prayed all night. When it was day, He called His twelve disciples unto Him, and a great multitude of people out of Judea, Jerusalem, Tyre, and Sidon came to hear Him, and to be healed. It was during this setting that the Messiah, the King, began to speak the great sermon that has been so misunderstood over the centuries.

The King was not giving the plan of salvation, as many have said, but He is giving them the *characteristics* of a person who is in His kingdom. So the King flings open the gates of His kingdom and lets them see what it is like.

The kingdom of God is not like the religious system that the people were used to hearing and seeing. This Kingdom would be given to the true, the humble, the poor in spirit, the meek, the ones who were thirsting after righteousness. The religious people of the day were hypocrites, taking advantage of the poor, taking advantage of the women, lovers of money, trying to justify themselves before men with their outward religious deeds. There were no Pharisees there that day, or they would have left. It was the common people from all around hearing Jesus preach about His kingdom.

Galilee was a place of revolt, and the Zealots who hid in the mountains were always fighting the Romans for their freedom. But here comes the Messiah, and His kingdom would not be won by force, but by love and forgiveness. The Old Testament began with the Ten Commandments, but the New Testament begins with the

Sermon on the Mount. The old said, "Thou shalt not," but the new said, "Blessed art thou."

It was not a matter of who was good, or who was pure within themselves, but it was those who believed that Jesus of Nazareth was the Messiah who would inherit the kingdom. It was all about the King living inside of His people, changing them into Kingdom children. Once a person is made new by the power of the Messiah, then they will love their enemies, they will give of their money. They will not judge others, they will not divorce their wives over little reasons. They won't just *say* the name of the Lord, but they will *do* what he says. The gate is much more narrow than what many have believed. Most people will go the broad way of destruction, but Jesus leads people on the narrow road to eternal life. They will either build their house on the sand or on the rock.

The kingdom of God, *mal choot Eloheem*, would be offered to whosoever will, or *mee sheh rotzeh sheh yavo*, "whosoever will may come." That day on the hillsides of Galilee, Jesus the Messiah was not offering the people a school or a religious system, He was offering them himself!

The Christ:

THE CENTURION'S SERVANT HEALED

Matthew 8:5–13   After the Sermon on the Mount, Jesus came down to Capernaum again, where He lived in the house of Andrew and Peter. The Messiah walked these very cobbled streets during the early first century.

Here is recorded the miracle of Jesus healing the centurion's servant. The centurion had come to believe in the God of Israel, and had built them a synagogue. He was called "a God-fearer," like Cornelius in Acts 10. This centurion came sincerely to Jesus, telling Him about his servant who was at home sick with the palsy. When Jesus told him that He would come and heal him, the centurion showed great humility. "Lord, I am not worthy that thou shouldest come under my roof: but speak the word only, and my servant shall be healed."

When Jesus saw the faith of the Gentile centurion He said, "Verily I say unto you, I have not found so great faith, no, not in Israel. And I say unto you, that many shall come from the east and west, and shall sit down with Abraham, and Isaac, and Jacob, in the kingdom of heaven. But the children of the kingdom shall be cast out into outer darkness: there shall be weeping and gnashing of teeth."

Here, we can see a prophecy of the Messiah. The promise that God made to Abraham, that all of the nations of the earth would be blessed through His seed, would come not only to the Jews, but to the rest of the world. The unbelief of the Jews would launch that promise of blessing to the Gentiles (Rom. 11). The Messiah came to His own people, to His own country, and was rejected, so He would graft in the Gentiles, and they would "no more be strangers and foreigners, but fellow citizens with the saints, and of the household of God" (Eph. 2:19).

This Roman centurion showed more faith in the Jewish Messiah than the "children of the kingdom." Many of the Jews would be lost, and many Gentiles would be saved. Jesus healed the centurion's servant because of his faith. When someone expressed true faith in Jesus as the Messiah in the gospels, miracles happened. The same is true today!

THE WOMEN DISCIPLES

Luke 8:1–3 — Jesus went throughout every city and village in Galilee preaching the kingdom of God with his 12 disciples, "and certain women" who had been healed of "evil spirits and infirmities" followed Him. The Scriptures name three of them here. Mary Magdalene, *Miryam Magdalit*, out of whom went seven demons; Joanna, *Yochanah*, the wife of Chuza, Herod's steward; and Susanna, *Shoshanah*. The Scriptures say there were "many others."

These women would not have traveled with the men disciples, but they would have followed in the distance. They helped finance the ministry of Jesus the Messiah. In the days of Jesus, women were looked at with contempt, and were very mistreated. Here we can see that after they met Jesus, their hearts were changed and they became great servants.

Magdala was a town on the northern shore of Galilee, noted for its industry, such as dye works and the manufacturing of fine woolen textures. It had hundreds of shops that sold pigeons and turtledoves for sacrifice. Wagon loads were carried to Jerusalem each year to the feasts. The road that brought Jesus into the plain of Gennesaret was between two mountains, called the "Valley of the Doves." Properly named because of the numerous doves that came out of Magdala, it was also a place of great immorality, and to this the rabbis attributed its final destruction. Here is the home town of Mary Magdala. She loved Jesus so much that she became one of His most devout disciples, as we will see later at the garden tomb.

Joanna, the wife of Chuza, had been so changed by Jesus that she was taking some of the money that her husband made working for

King Herod Antipas, and giving it to Jesus. Wow! Even King Herod was funding the Messiah's ministry, and didn't know it.

We find that these women followed Jesus all the way to the Cross in Jerusalem. What a great lesson for us to learn. Where would the modern-day Church be without godly women? Because of our traditions, we still push the women aside in many cases. But the Scriptures tell us that Jesus showed compassion on the women of His day, and many of them became great heralds of the gospel. Jesus was a revolutionary who not only included Gentiles in His kingdom, but women as well.

The Lord is looking for servants. The word "servant" in Hebrew is *eved*. There is neither male nor female in Christ Jesus (Gal. 3:28). The Lord has a plan for the men to lead their families, and be spiritual leaders in the church, but He also has a place for godly women, and may we never forget it! I once read Luke 8:1–3 to a group while in Israel, and many said, "I never knew that passage was in the Bible." I'm afraid there are many things that people do not know are in the Bible.

JUDGMENT PREDICTED

Matthew 11:20–30 Here we can easily see that there are different degrees of punishment. The cities of Chorazin *(Korazin)*, Bethsaida *(Beit-Tzaidah)*, and Capernaum *(K'far-Nachum)* would suffer more at the Day of Judgment than the cities of Tyre and Sidon, which were Gentile cities in the north. Also, Jesus said that even Sodom *(S'Dom)* in the Old Testament that was destroyed by fire and brimstone would not suffer as much as Capernaum. Now what does all this mean?

Jesus the Messiah lived in Capernaum; He performed most of His miracles in the three cities mentioned above. The people had the very Son of God walking in their streets. Many of the people rejected Him as the Messiah. The leaders in the synagogues called Jesus a blasphemer, and they ran Him out of their places of worship. His ministry started in the synagogues, then He had to go to the highways and hillsides around Galilee. Although many believed in Jesus as the Messiah, most of Israel did not know Him when He came. The more light that is given, the more responsibility is required. When they heard and saw the Messiah, they were required to believe in Him, and they did not. As Jesus said later, "Some will be beaten with many stripes, and some with few."

Jesus gave us a great lesson in verse 25: "At that time Jesus answered and said, I thank thee, O Father, Lord of heaven and earth, because thou hast hid these things from the wise and prudent, and hast revealed them unto babes." Religion places people in bondage, and blinds them from the Messiah. They were praying, tithing, and attending services, but did not know their King when He came. The

Kingdom is revealed to child-like people, the humble, not the self-righteous, pious people.

This is a pivotal point in the ministry of the Messiah. The Kingdom will not come to Israel at this time, because they have rejected their King. So here Jesus turns to the common people, and offers them peace and rest for their souls after being placed under religious bondage by their leaders. "Come unto me, all ye that labour and are heavy laden, and I will give you rest. Take *my* yoke upon you, and learn of *me*; for I am meek and lowly in heart; and ye shall find rest for your souls. For *my* yoke is easy, and *my* burden is light." Serving God is not supposed to be a burden on anybody — it is a joy. Coming to the Messiah, one finds true rest and true peace. No doubt Jesus had made many yokes when He was growing up in Nazareth as a carpenter. Here He uses that illustration to show that when we are yoked with Him, we will grow and learn how to serve in His kingdom. The people were oppressed, even by the ones who were supposed to be their spiritual leaders. The nation had become just a place of man-made traditions, and the sincere people had no one to lead them.

What a warning this is for all of us. We should beware when our church becomes a drudgery, and when the joy begins to leave. We are to be serving Christ with joy and gladness. Where His Spirit is, there is liberty. So many who think they are doing all the right things will be lost in the end. Only the children of God will have eternal life. Judgment will be severe for those who have heard the gospel and have rejected it. We will be surprised one day to find out that the real servants of the Lord were not religious, they were believers in Messiah!

The Parables

1) THE HEBREW PROPHECIES

"Give ear, O my people, to my law; incline your ears to the words of my mouth. I will open my mouth in a parable; I will utter dark sayings of old: which we have heard and known, and our fathers have told us. We will not hide them from their children, shewing to the generation to come the praises of the LORD, and his strength, and his wonderful works that he hath done" (Ps. 78:1–4).

The word "parable" in Hebrew is *mashal*. It was prophesied that the coming Messiah would speak in parables. This was also a style of teaching that was used by many of the Jewish rabbis. So one of the reasons Jesus spoke in parables was to fulfill prophecy.

2) THE HISTORICAL SITUATION

History

Matthew 13 The Jewish establishment in Matthew 12 had condemned Jesus and said that His miracles were the workings of Satan. They condemned Jesus for plucking some ears of corn on the Sabbath day and for healing a man with a withered hand on the Sabbath day. Then when He cast the demons out of a man, they said He was doing it by the power of Beelzebub. They committed the *unpardonable sin!* Jesus said they were clean on the outside, but corrupt on the inside. Jesus closes chapter 12 by saying that His true family are the ones who do the will of His Father. Just being a Jew or just being in His earthly family was not enough — powerful words, but words that we all need to hear.

So the Kingdom was not going to come to Israel. The offer had been made and rejected. Now Jesus begins to speak in parables. Why?

Matt. 13:10–17 Jesus spoke in parables to reveal the mysteries of the Kingdom to the believers, and to conceal the mysteries of the Kingdom from the unbelievers. The disciples and many others in the first century were very blessed to hear and see the Messiah himself. They were given things that even the prophets were not given. But many of the Pharisees had turned a deaf ear to Jesus, and now Jesus turns from them. It was in the springtime, and Yeshua sat in a boat, while multitudes were standing on the shore.

3) THE SPIRITUAL APPLICATION

Eight great parables were given in Matthew 13. That makes it one of the greatest chapters in the Gospel accounts. Jesus gave many other parables — over 35 are recorded — but we will just look at this chapter for now.

1) *The parable of the sower* (Matt. 13:1–9, 18–23): Using the familiar scene of a farmer who was sowing his seed that day in the fields near by, the Messiah was telling them what to expect when they went out preaching God's Word. These mysteries would occur during the church age.

Application

Some would hear the message of the Kingdom, but never be able to understand it *(seeds that fell by the wayside, and Satan came and snatched the Word out of their hearts).*

Some would hear the message of the Kingdom and joyfully receive it, but when they discovered that it was difficult to live the Christian life, they would drop out *(seeds that fell on stony ground).*

Some would hear the message of the kingdom, but the cares of the world and the love of riches would choke out the word *(seeds that fell among the thorns).*

Some would hear the Word and understand it, and go and bring forth fruit, some a hundredfold, some sixty, some thirty *(seeds that fell on the good ground).*

2) *The parable of the tares and the wheat* (Matt. 13:24–30): The Kingdom would have the true and the false. The true would be planted there by God, and the false would be planted by Satan. It would not be our job to separate them, because sometimes we cannot tell who is real and who is not. But one day the Lord will separate the false from the true. We can see this in our day. Many learn the church talk and act out the part, but they are not the children of God. Our job is to just keep on serving the Lord, and not be the judge.

3) *The parable of the grain of mustard seed* (Matt. 13:31–32): The kingdom would experience a supernatural growth, like a little mustard seed becoming a big tree. When the birds saw the tree, they would come and lodge in its branches. Jesus was probably talking about evil lodging in the branches of the Kingdom. This seems to match the other parables.

4) *The parable of the leaven* (Matt. 13:33): Leaven is a picture of sin or hypocrisy in the Bible, normally, but here I believe Jesus is just using it to illustrate that the Kingdom would permeate the entire world. If He was talking about leaven in the evil sense, we can see that false doctrine has spread throughout the Church world as well.

5) *The parable of the hidden treasure* (Matt. 13:44): In the time of Jesus, it was very common for a farmer to be plowing his field and overturn a pot of coins that maybe someone had buried to keep the Romans from getting. If that man went and bought the field, the treasure would belong to him. Jesus was saying that when we see how valuable the kingdom of heaven is, we will give up everything else to be a part of it. We cannot buy salvation, but Jesus was showing the wonder and amazement of finding the Kingdom, and how a person would respond. The devil blinds people to how marvelous God's kingdom really is.

6) *The parable of the pearl of great price* (Matt. 13:45–46): The main caravan route that ran through Galilee was called the "Via Maris," and it ran just north of Capernaum. The village people were used to hearing the merchant men talk about their wish to find that one pearl of great price. Pearls were common, but that special pearl was worth more than all the rest put together. When that merchant man found that one priceless pearl, he would go and sell all his possessions just to purchase it. The kingdom of heaven is like that, in the sense that when we see its glory and splendor, how eternal it is, how beautiful it is, we will make it our top priority in life. The Kingdom is not just an addition to our lives, it *is* our lives, once we see it for what it really is.

7) *The parable of the drag net* (Matt. 13:47–50): There were several different ways to fish in the time of Jesus. One was to use what was called "the drag net." This method could be used by one or two boats. Sometimes several men would hold the end of a huge net on the shore, while men in a boat would circle a large area, and then pull the net back to the shore. With weights on the bottom of the net, it would catch everything in its pathway, from top to bottom. Sometimes they would bring in rocks and water snakes. The fish they caught were either good or bad. The bad fish were the ones that did not have scales, in this case, catfish. Catfish were not lawful to eat. So here Jesus is talking about something that all the common people knew that lived in Galilee. This was very similar to the parable of the tares and the wheat. The Kingdom would have good and bad, and just like when they threw the catfish away, one day the bad would be cast away into everlasting punishment. The Kingdom attracts all kinds of charlatans, false prophets, and shysters. But we can be assured that they will not get away from God's all-seeing eyes.

8) *The parable of the householder* (Matt. 13:52): A scribe was someone who studied and copied down the old Hebrew Scriptures. When he was taught about the kingdom of heaven, he was like a man who was a householder, who brought forth out of his house treasures new and old. By this time, Jesus had sent the multitude away, and was now in a house (verse 36). This meant that the scribe would see that Jesus of Nazareth was the Messiah that the old Hebrew Scriptures talked about. He would see the treasures in the old, and the treasures in the new. The fulfillment of those Scriptures would be opened up to Him.

Those people who were there that day would have told their families and friends about Yeshua the Messiah. Try to imagine what it must have been like to have heard Jesus teaching on the shore of the Sea of Galilee. We need to make sure that we are children of that Kingdom.

In Song

Such Is the Kingdom of Heaven

Such is the kingdom of heaven,
Such is the kingdom of God.
Such is the kingdom of heaven,
Such is the kingdom of God.

Just like the sower that went forth to sow —
Some fell by the way,
Some fell among stony ground,
Some fell among thorns,
Some fell among good ground,
That's how the kingdom is born.

Just like the mustard seed that's so small,
It will grow beyond compare.
Just like the leaven hid in the meal,
The kingdom will spread every where.

Just like the tares that grow with the wheat,
Only God can tell.
For the treasure hid in the field,
Everything a man would sell.

Such is the kingdom of heaven,
Such is the kingdom of God.
Such is the kingdom of heaven,
Such is the kingdom of God.

For the pearl of great price,
A man would give anything.
Just like the net with the good fish and bad,
Judgment will come with the King.

Such is the kingdom of heaven,
Such is the kingdom of God.
Such is the kingdom of heaven,
Such is the kingdom of God.

Written by Carroll Roberson. Copyright: Jesus Is Real Music (BMI)

A GREAT DAY IN THE LIFE OF MESSIAH

Mark 4:35–5:20 According to the Gospel of Mark, after the Messiah had ended His parabolic teaching on the shores of Galilee, the night was drawing near. He told the disciples to get into a boat and pass over to the other side. While they were out on the lake, a great storm arose, so much that water was filling up the ship. North of the Sea of Galilee, Mount Hermon rises to over 9,000 feet above sea level. The cold air from the mountains rushes down and meets the warm air at Galilee, which is over 650 feet below sea level. This can create a great storm in a matter of minutes. Jesus was asleep, with His head resting on one of the floating cushions in the boat.

What a picture, the King of the universe, asleep in a little boat. The disciples were so afraid and they cried out, "Master, carest thou not that we perish?" Jesus arose and rebuked the sea the same way He had rebuked the demons. He said, "Peace be still, and the wind ceased, and there was a great calm." Imagine a man speaking to the wind. Jesus the Messiah talked to the wind. Not only did the wind cease, but the water was as quiet as a piece of glass. When the Master of the sea speaks, everything obeys. I can't help but think of the verse in Psalm 107:29, "He maketh the storm a calm, so that the waves thereof are still." And the verse in Psalm 93: 4, "The Lord on high is mightier than the noise of many waters, yea, than the mighty waves of the sea."

Jesus asked His disciples, "Why are ye so fearful? How is it that ye have no faith? And they feared exceedingly, and said one to another, what manner of man is this, that even the wind and the sea obey him?" How would you feel, if you realized that God was standing in your boat out on the sea? He was the God-man — 100 percent God, and 100 percent man. Great is the mystery!

We need to see that our Savior has power over the natural elements of our lives. The one who calmed the storm can certainly take care of our problems. He may not always calm the storm in our lives, but He will calm us while we go through the storm, if we will trust Him and let Him have control. He loves us just as much as He did those disciples. He truly is "Jehovah Shalom," the Lord of peace!

Mark 5:1–20 When one goes to Galilee, they see on the eastern shore a place called Kursi. This place has a steep cliff where there were tombs in the time of Jesus. The old Hebrew scholar Alfred Edersheim says that when Jesus and the disciples got to this place, it was still night. And like many other places Jesus traveled throughout His earthly ministry, demons cried out when the Son of God arrived. There was a man living in the tombs who was suicidal. He had no self-control, and could not be controlled by anyone else. He was a man so bound by the powers of hell that he broke chains, and was constantly cutting himself and crying out from the tombs.

When he saw Jesus, he ran and worshiped Him, and cried with a loud voice, "What have I to do with thee, Jesus, thou Son of the most high God?" (Mark 5:7; Luke 8:28). It's amazing that the demons knew who Jesus was and many humans did not. Jesus commanded the demon to come out of the man, and asked him his name. He said, "My name is legion, for we are many" (Mark 5:9). This conveyed the idea of 6,000 armed and strong warriors of evil.

The demons began to beg Jesus to send them into a herd of swine who were feeding on the mountains. About 2,000 pigs ran violently down the cliff and were drowned in the sea. The people who fed the swine went and told the people in the city what had happened. They came and saw the man in his right mind, fully clothed, sitting at the feet of Jesus. They became afraid, and they began to pray that Jesus would depart out of their territory. People will either come to Jesus, or they will turn Him away.

When Jesus and the disciples got back into the ship, the man wanted to go with Jesus, but Jesus told him to go back home and tell what great things God had done for him. He went throughout all of the Decapolis and told them what Jesus had done for him. We will see the results of what he did a little later.

This story tells us that only the Messiah can defeat Satan. Many of the Jewish people in Jesus' day thought that storms were caused by the powers of darkness. If that were so, then both the storm and the possessed man were direct confrontations with the devil. Jesus, the Son of God, defeated them then, and He would defeat them later, and He will always be the Lord God Almighty! One of the most common names for God in Hebrew is *Elohim*, the All-Powerful Creator!

RAISING JAIRUS'S DAUGHTER AND HEALING THE WOMAN WITH AN ISSUE OF BLOOD

Mark 5:21–43   It's beautiful to see the power of the Messiah out on the Sea of Galilee and His power casting out the demons from the maniac of Gadara, and then to see what happens when people put their faith in the Messiah when He arrives back on the other side at Capernaum. It is also interesting to note that the people on the eastern shore asked Him to leave their midst, and when He came back to Capernaum He found a multitude waiting for Him.

When He got on the shore, a ruler of the synagogue, Jairus, *Ya'ir*, came and fell at His feet. He had heard of and seen the miracles of this man Jesus before, so he told Him of his 12-year-old daughter, who was at the point of death. He prayed that the Lord would come and lay His hands on her that she would live.

Here we have a marvelous scene of Jesus going with this man, and the multitude following. While on the way to the home of Jairus, a woman pressed her way through the crowd and touched His garment. She had an issue of blood for 12 years, and had spent all her living on physicians, but was getting worse. (See the Jewish law concerning a woman with an issue of blood, Lev. 15:25–31). Everything she touched was unclean, and if she touched another person, they were unclean until night, and they had to even wash their clothes.

No doubt, Jesus wore a prayer shawl called a *tallit*, which had four corners with fringes on each corner (Num. 15:38–41; Deut. 22:12). These tassels were to remind the Jewish men to keep the Law, and to be holy for God. She touched the fringes of his *tallit*, saying that she believed that He was the long-awaited Messiah. One of the prophecies concerning the coming Messiah is Malachi 4:2, "But unto you that fear my name shall the Sun of righteousness arise with healing in his wings." The Messiah is the "Sun of righteousness," and He will have healing in his "wings," or *tzit tzit.* This woman believed that the Messiah had come, and His name was *Yeshua min Notzri,* Jesus of Nazareth. She was immediately made whole, because of her faith in the Messiah (verse 34).

While Jesus was speaking to the woman, some people came to Him from the home of Jairus and told Him that there was no need to bother, the little girl was already dead. But Jesus told Jairus, "Be not afraid, only believe." He took Peter, James, and John with Him. When they came to the house, Jesus saw all the people weeping and He said, "Why make ye this ado, and weep? The damsel is not dead, but sleepeth." After Jesus made the people leave, we have a very touching picture. Jesus took the father and the mother, and went to the bedside of the little girl. He took her by the hand and said, *"Talitha cumi,"* which means, "Damsel, I say unto thee arise." The word *talitha* is a feminine lamb. So He was saying, "Little lamb, arise."

What compassion we see here in the Messiah. The little girl arose immediately and walked. She was 12 years of age, the same amount of years that the woman had had the issue of blood. Then Jesus commanded them to give her something to eat. The precious Savior wanted the parents to have the joy of seeing their little girl eating again. Jesus was always concerned about His people having something to eat in the Gospels. The Hebrew word for "life" is *chay.* One of the words that describes *chay* is "appetite." Yeshua was showing that the little girl really was alive; she could eat again.

So what do these miracles mean to us today? They show us that Jesus the Messiah came to give us life and life more abundantly. If we put our faith in Jesus the Messiah, we shall live forever. He is the only hope we have, but what a hope that is. We all have the sentence of death upon us, but Jesus came to reverse that sentence. As the great apostle Paul wrote about 30 years later, "If in this life only we have hope in Christ, we are of all men most miserable."

THE FEEDING OF
THE FIVE THOUSAND

Mark 6:32–44 Jesus had gone back to Nazareth, where many of His own people rejected Him. Jesus left us a tremendous lesson when He said, "A prophet is not without honour, but in his own country, and among his own kin, and in his own house." Then He sent the 12 disciples out to preach, two by two. He also gave them the power to heal and to cast out demons. He told them to carry only a staff, and when the people did not receive them, to shake the dust off their feet. When they came back to Jesus after their first preaching tour, a great crowd of people were thronging around them, so Jesus told them to get away, and rest a while. They didn't even have time to eat, Jesus said.

By this time, John the Baptist had been murdered by the wicked King Herod, and the people were following Jesus now more than ever. So Jesus and His disciples departed from the northern shore by ship, and sailed over to the eastern side to Bethsaida, *Beit-Tzaidah*, which means, "house of fishing." The great crowd of people outran Jesus and His disciples on the hillsides. They were already there when Jesus arrived, and He saw them as sheep not having a shepherd, and was moved with compassion. What a contrast between King Herod killing John the Baptist, and King Jesus having compassion on the multitude. We know that, according to John's gospel, it was approaching the Jewish feast of Passover, which was in the springtime. This explains why there was grass on the hillsides. I have been to Israel many times during the spring, and it is beautiful when the grass around Galilee is green on the hillsides.

As the day was growing closer to night, the disciples asked Jesus to send the people away, so they would have time to go into the towns and buy some bread. This is when Jesus took the lunch from the little boy, which was five loaves of bread and two fishes. The bread was round and flat, and John's Gospel tells us that it was barley, the poorest means in those days. The fishes were the small, pickled, sardine-size *opsarion*. Jesus looked up to heaven and gave thanks, and we know what the Jewish blessing was: *"Baruch ata Adonai Eloheynu melech haholam hahmotzee lechem meen hah eretz,"* which means "Blessed are you, O Lord our God, King of the universe that bringeth forth bread from the earth." Five thousand men, not counting the women and children, ate and were filled that afternoon. And they took up 12 *kophinoy*, small wicker baskets, of fragments. Remember the *opsarion* and the *kophinoy* for we will hear about them again later.

The Christ:

Now what does all this mean to us today? It means that we serve a Messiah who is filled with compassion, and He is concerned about our daily needs. And it shows that no matter how little we may feel, and how little we may have, God seems to make little things go a long way. As we look at the Scriptures, we find David killing Goliath with only a rock and a sling. We see Gideon defeating the thousands of Midianites, not with 22,000 men, but with only 300 men. Why does the Lord do things this way? To show that the power is in Christ, and not within ourselves. God chose planet Earth out of all the universe for people to inhabit. He chose the Jewish people to be the race to bring forth the Messiah. He chose the little nation of Israel to be the place where the Messiah would be born. He chose to start the kingdom of God with the outcast people of Galilee. Now, look at how far the message of the Messiah has gone. God uses the simple things to confound the wise (1 Cor. 1:26–28).

But more importantly, this miracle shows that the Messiah was the fulfillment of the manna that came down from heaven to feed the children of Israel in the wilderness. John 6:22–5 tells us that Jesus taught in the synagogue in Capernaum the next day, "I am the bread of life," *"Anee hoo lehem hachaim."* All who believe in the Messiah will never die. He came down from heaven to give us eternal life. We will be satisfied when we "Taste and see that the Lord is good" (Ps. 34:8). I rejoice that Yeshua had compassion for the multitude that day, and I rejoice that Yeshua had compassion for me!

Bread of Life

Jesus took five loaves and two fishes
    fed five thousand at Galilee.
He is the true manna from heaven
    He came down to feed you and me.

The Bread of Life for you and I,
The only One who can satisfy.
Messiah, Messiah, the Bread of Life.

To the men, women, and children
    who taste of Messiah today,
They will never, never more hunger
    and their life will never pass away.

The Bread of Life for you and I,
The only One who can satisfy.
Messiah, Messiah, the Bread of Life.

Written by Carroll Roberson and Nathan Wood. Copyright: Jesus Is Real Music (BMI)

Jesus Walks on the Sea

Mark 6:45–52 Probably the most vivid picture I get in my mind when we travel to the Sea of Galilee is the supernatural miracle of Jesus the Messiah walking on the sea. One cannot look across the water without almost seeing Jesus stepping across the waves. I have been on the sea when it was rocky, and my mind would go back to that disciple-changing night, when it all happened.

Jesus had just fed thousands on the eastern shore, and He told the disciples to get into the boat and cross back over to Bethsaida. We must not get confused, there were two towns called Bethsaida, one on the east, and one on the northwestern shore. After the Messiah sent them away, He departed to a mountain to pray. While Jesus was on the mountain, He saw the disciples toiling and rowing in the midst of the sea. It was about four o'clock in the morning, and Jesus came to them, walking on the water, and made as though He "would have passed by them." The disciples thought they had seen a spirit, and they cried out. But Jesus being the Prince of Peace, startled talking to them and said, "Be of good cheer; it is I; be not afraid."

When Jesus got into the ship, the wind ceased, and wonder filled the disciples. For they had forgotten about the miracle that had just happened a few hours before, when Jesus fed the multitude. John's Gospel tells us that "immediately the ship was back on the shore," an overlooked miracle within itself.

The Scriptures tell us that when they arrived back at the land of Gennesaret, which is on the north-western shore, people who were sick started coming to Him from everywhere. It must have been a sight to see, people carrying sick people in beds, sick people lying in the streets, and Jesus healed them.

So what do all these miracles mean to us today?

1) THE HEBREW SCRIPTURES

Psalm 77:19 "Thy way is in the sea, and thy path in the great waters, and thy footsteps are not known." Job 9:8: "Which alone spreadeth out the heavens, and treadeth upon the waves of the sea." All of the Scriptures, the *Tanach* and *Brit Hadasha*, Old Testament and New Testament, are woven together like a beautiful piece of tapestry. We see the same God in the old as we do in the new. Jesus the Messiah proved that He was the God of the Old Testament. His path was in the waters, and people just don't walk on water, but Jesus did. The same God that parted the waters of the mighty Red Sea came in the form of a man in Jesus the Messiah. In the time of Jesus, many of the rabbis believed the sea was a symbol of evil, and Jesus not only cast out evil from people, but He walked on evil as well.

2) SPIRITUAL LESSON #1

Matthew's Gospel tells us that Simon Peter, *Shimon Kefa*, also walked on the water to go to Jesus. Peter knew the sea very well; he wasn't trying to be cute or perform magic. He was so in awe of Jesus, that he wanted to be with Him, and walking on water didn't seem impossible as long as he kept his eyes on Jesus. It was only when he saw the waves, that he started to sink. What a great lesson for all of us who profess the name of Yeshua. We can experience the supernatural, as long as we are focusing on Christ. It's when we start looking at the problems around us that we get into trouble. Matthew 14:33 says, "Then they that were in the ship came and worshiped him, saying, Of a truth thou art the Son of God." Worship in Hebrew is *shachah*, which means to "prostrate, bow down, or fall down." Try to imagine the scene, in the middle of the Sea of Galilee, with all of the disciples falling down in the boat giving worship to the Christ! It's interesting also to go back to Exodus 14 and 15, when God destroyed the Egyptians in the Red Sea, with the breath of His nostrils. The Scriptures say it was in the "morning watch" when it happened. Could there be any connection to Jesus walking on the water during the "morning watch"? As God redeemed the children of Israel from Egyptian bondage, the Messiah came to redeem us out of the bondage of sin!

3) SPIRITUAL LESSON #2

Our Lord is a strange person sometimes, and He does strange things. Here He made them think He was going to pass them by. He had no intentions of passing them by, but He made them think that so they would cry out for Him. We will see this strange action again a little later, after the Resurrection. This tells us that the Lord may allow us to feel far away from Him at times, or we wonder what in the world is going on in our Christian life. But He is wanting our fellowship, our love and trust. I know this may sound a little ridiculous, but sometimes I think the Lord gets lonely. He loves us so much, that He wants us to acknowledge Him in all we do. And once we find out who He is, and that there is nothing to be afraid of, we will!

4) SPIRITUAL LESSON #3

If the disciples had remembered what Jesus did on the shore a few hours earlier, it would have saved them a lot of worry. Maybe Jesus was trying to teach them how to serve Him, when He was *not* in the boat with them. He had already calmed the storm when He was with them; this time was different. We get into spiritual trouble when we forget what Christ has already done for us. Do you think that after He came from heaven, died on a cross, and rose again, for our sins, that He will leave us alone in our earthly lives? Not for one minute! He will never leave us and never forsake us, and may we never forget that!

5) SPIRITUAL LESSON #4

Jesus healed people everywhere He went, when He walked this earth. Jesus healed people because of His great compassion, and to show that He was the one and only Messiah. And no matter what our theology may be, whether we believe in dispensationalism or not (I personally hold to a mild dispensational perspective), we need to have the faith to ask Him for help, believing without doubt that He can and will heal us today. Our faith is *not* in miracles, but in the person of Messiah. We serve an awesome God, *Jehovah Rapha*, "The Lord Who Heals!" The One who walked on water can certainly take care of us. The lesson the disciples learned is certainly one for us today — truly, Jesus is the Son of God!

The Feeding of the Four Thousand

Mark 8:1–9   To bring you up to date on what has transpired in the life of Messiah, when you go to Capernaum today, you will find not only the ruins of a synagogue that stands on the foundations of the one Jesus taught in, but you can see the remains of some of the carvings that were over the entrance door of the synagogue. One of the carvings is a pot of manna, which symbolizes what God had done in the Old Testament, and also what the Messiah offers in the New. After He gave that stirring discourse in the synagogue at Capernaum on the bread of life, many of His so-called disciples left Him. That's always the case when people are following the Lord for the wrong reasons. But Peter and the Twelve realized that they could not go back to their old jobs, and that Jesus was the only one who had eternal life.

The window of opportunity for the Messiah to travel and preach His message was closing little by little. He knew what the hour was on the clock, and He was moving from place to place more now than before. The Pharisees were hot on His trail, condemning Him and trying to find fault in Him. When they couldn't find anything, they would accuse Him of not washing His hands before He ate. How sad. The religious people needed cleansing on the inside, and they were condemning the only one who *could* cleanse them for having dirty hands.

But may we never forget that multitudes of the common people loved Jesus, and His ministry had grown to an enormous following by now. So Jesus, not wanting to hinder His heaven-sent mission, knew that He must be wise with His time. He departed northward to the land of Tyre and Sidon. While there, He found a Syrophoenician woman who realized that she is just a "dog," Gentile (Mark 7:24–30). But because of her great faith, He healed her daughter. The Messiah was sent to the lost sheep of the house of Israel, but He always showed mercy to anyone who believed in Him.

Then traveling back southward, He went back through the Decapolis, and healed a man who was deaf and dumb. Oh, how we take for granted those everyday blessings, such as being able to hear and to talk. May we use our God-given faculties for His glory.

While in the land of the Decapolis, "ten cities," He fed a multitude of people once again. His previous miracle of feeding the 5,000 was with the Jews of Galilee. Now, He was with the Gentiles, in a different region. It seems to me worth noting that Jesus seemed to always be eating with people. Eating was a sign of forgiveness in the first century, and the Messiah loved to see people enjoying life, especially when it was with Him. When Jesus cast the demons out of the maniac of Gadara in Mark 5, He told him to go home and tell others what God had done for him. So he went throughout all of the Decapolis and spread the news about Yeshua, and in a few short weeks, look what happened. No doubt, that man helped to bring the great multitude to Jesus when He passed through the second time.

Also, church history tells us that many Christian churches sprang up in that region in later years, as a result of this man's witness. What a tremendous difference one person can make, when they experience the power of the Messiah.

There are several distinctions about the two feedings. The first was *5,000*, the second was *4,000*. At the first feeding they had *five* loaves of bread, at the second they had *seven*. At the first they had *12* baskets left over, the second they had *7* baskets left over. At the first feeding they gathered up the fragments in *small* wicker baskets, *kophinoy*, which were Jewish baskets. At the second feeding, they gathered up the fragments with *large* baskets, *spryidas*, which were Gentile baskets with handles.

There is something very powerful about the two feedings symbolically. It is interesting to mention that some think the 12 baskets left over during the first feeding symbolize the 12 tribes of Israel, and the 7 baskets left over during the second feeding symbolize the 7 heathen peoples that should have been driven out in the time of Joshua — the Canaanites, the Hittites, the Hivites, the Perizzites, the Girgashites, the Amorites, and the Jebusites. One of them, the Girgashites, had settled back into this region during the time of Jesus. This feeding probably included the Girgashites, symbolizing the ministry of the Messiah toward the Gentiles and the beginning of the Messianic age. The gates of the kingdom were open for the Jews and the Gentiles.

These two miracles show that Yahweh, the God of the Bible, had provided Yeshua, the Messiah, for all people. It's important to know the proper name for God, because in His name is salvation. Not in the name of *Iesous*, or Jesus, but *Yeshua*, which comes from the name *Yahweh*. One of the names of God in Hebrew is *Jehovah Jireh*, "the Lord will provide."

THE GREAT CONFESSION

Matthew 16: 13–18　　As we search the gospels, we see that Jesus and His disciples left the land of the Decapolis, the land southeast of the Sea of Galilee, after the feeding of the four thousand, and came back across the lake to Magdala, or as Mark's gospel says, Dalmanutha. Both are the same area northwest of the Sea of Galilee, Dalmanutha being a little bay within that area. When the Pharisees, along with the Sadducees, came tempting Jesus, they departed *again* in a ship to go back across to the eastern shore. While they were in the ship, the disciples had forgotten to take any bread with them, and Jesus used that to teach them about the "leaven of the Pharisees." They finally understood that He was not talking about physical bread, but the hypocrisy of the Pharisees. They should have realized that the true "Bread of Life" was riding with them in the boat.

So the Galilean ministry of the Messiah is coming to a close, and the Messiah takes His disciples up north again, this time to the territory of Herod Philip, the brother of Herod Antipas, whose hands were blood-stained from the death of John the Baptist. The capital of Philip's territory was Paneas, where a Greek temple stood honoring the shepherd-like god, "Pan." Statues of this half-man, half-goat god were placed in niches in the rocky cliffs. Herod Philip beautified Paneas and named it after the emperor Caesar and himself, calling it Caesarea Philippi. After a two-day journey, Jesus and His disciples would have arrived.

In Mark 8:22–26, Jesus and the disciples came to the city of Bethsaida, where the people brought a blind man to Him. Jesus spit on his eyes. It was commonly thought in the time of Jesus that the spittle of the firstborn child had healing power. Jesus was the firstborn son of Mary, but He was also the first begotten Son of God! This miracle at Bethsaida was unique in the fact that the man could only see men "as trees walking" after Jesus touched him the first time. Jesus had to touch him the second time before he could see clearly. I ask you, dear reader, do you believe that Jesus could have healed him with the first touch? Of course He could have! But there was a message in the way He did the miracle for the disciples. Just as the blind man was not able to see clearly when Jesus first touched him, the disciples could not see everything clearly either at this point. They were learning, but it would take the death, burial, and resurrection of the Messiah to open their eyes clearly. Little by little, they were seeing who He was and why He came into the world.

What happened at Caesarea Philippi is of such vital importance that we must see the actual verses:

> When Jesus came into the coasts of Caesarea Philippi, He asked his disciples, saying, whom do men say that I the Son of man am? And they said, some say that thou art John the Baptist; some Elias; and others, Jeremias, or one of the prophets. He saith unto them, but whom say ye that I am? And Simon Peter answered and said, thou art the Christ, the Son of the Living God. And Jesus answered and said unto him, blessed art thou, Simon Bar-Jona; for flesh and blood hath not revealed it unto thee, but my Father which is in heaven. And I say unto thee, that thou art Peter, and upon this rock I will build my church; and the gates of hell shall not prevail against it.

So it is interesting that Jesus took the disciples far away from Jerusalem, the temple, the Pharisees, the Sadducees, and even Galilee, for this monumental event. The foundation that the church would be built upon was first confessed in a Gentile region.

Two questions that Jesus asked: "Whom do *men* say that I . . . am?" And, "Whom say *ye* that I am?" Some thought maybe because of His preaching on repentance, that He was John the Baptist. Some thought because of His power to raise the dead that He was Elijah.

Some thought because of the compassion of Jesus, that He was Jeremiah. Others didn't know, but they thought He was one of the Old Testament prophets. But the question that must have made the eyes of the disciples grow big was, "Whom say *ye* that I am?" Simon Peter burst forth, "Thou art the Messiah [Greek word is *Christ*], the son of the living God."

If they were going to confront the false gods of Rome and Greece, they must know *who* Jesus was. We know that the Father revealed to Peter who Jesus was, and Jesus called him "blessed." Each passing sermon that Jesus had preached, and each passing miracle that He had performed, were little by little opening the eyes of the disciples to *who* He was. An example is the miracle He performed on the blind man at Bethsaida. He touched the blind man once, and the man saw men as trees, walking. He touched him twice and the man could see clearly. The disciples were seeing more clearly, but they would encounter many other doubts and fears before they could see perfectly clearly.

Jesus said, "Thou art Peter, *petros* [little rock], and upon this rock, *petra*, I will build My church, *ecclesia*, [called out ones]." Contrary to what many think, Jesus was not saying that He was going to build His Church on Peter, but on the "big rock" confession that he had just made. The truth of Jesus of Nazareth being the Son of God would build the Church.

There are three things about the Church that we need to make clear:

1) The *Church* is not a building or a denomination, but it is God's people. In Hebrew it is *kahal*, the called-out people who belong to the Messiah. The Messiah would live in His people through the indwelling Holy Spirit.

2) The *Church* belongs to Jesus the Messiah — it is His. He will build the true Church. Most of what we have today is a man-made church, with man-made traditions.

3) The *Church* will not even be destroyed by death itself. The Messiah would die and rise again. His Church would stand all the persecutions of the centuries.

Jesus went on to tell Peter that he would have the keys of the Kingdom. Peter would later open the door to the Gentiles officially in the Book of Acts, to Cornelius, at Caesarea. Then Jesus began to openly talk about His death and resurrection in Jerusalem. And because of the disciples' lack of understanding, Satan tempted Jesus through Peter. Sometimes Satan uses our closest friends and family to tempt us. Jesus told them that they must take up their cross if they were going to follow Him. And they must realize that to be a good disciple, their minds must not be on worldly riches. Jesus closed the conversation by warning them that if a man gains the whole world, and loses his own soul, he's lost it all. Their reward would come later, and it would supercede anything the world had to offer.

THE MOUNT OF TRANSFIGURATION

Luke 9:27–36
Matthew 17:1–8
Mark 9:2–8

After that earth-shaking confession that Simon Peter had made, saying that Jesus was the Messiah, the Son of God, we realize how important it was to the disciples and the course of history. For if Jesus was not the Messiah, the Son of God, then He was just a reformer, just a rabbi, just a religious teacher. But throughout the centuries, it has been proven over and over again that Jesus truly is who He claimed to be. This is the foundation of the Christian gospel.

Then He told the disciples, that *some* of them (referring to James, Peter, and John) would not see death until they saw the kingdom of God. This was referring to what was about to happen. I believe the Mount of Transfiguration is probably the most overlooked moment in the life of Jesus Christ. Maybe it's because we, too, do not fully understand the power and the glory of this heavenly event.

First of all, let me say that it is thought by many that the Transfiguration occurred on Mount Tabor, several miles south of Galilee. This is not likely, because during this time there was a fortified city on top of Mount Tabor. Also, Jesus and His disciples were already in the vicinity of the tallest mountain in Israel, Mount Hermon, which stands over 9,000 feet above sea level. Now, it probably happened on one of the mountains close by Mount Hermon, about eight days after the great confession of Peter.

The same three disciples who were there at Jairus's house, James, Peter, and John, would go with Jesus to the mountain to pray.

Jesus was transfigured before them, and the only thing that could describe the *shechinah* glory was the white snow of Mount Hermon, or the brightness of the sun, as Matthew's Gospel tells us. The deity of the Messiah broke through for a short glimpse into the future.

There were, standing with Him on the mountain, two of the great Old Testament men, *Moshe* and *Eliyahu*, which is Hebrew for Moses and Elijah. Why were they there? They represented the *Law* and the *Prophets*. What were they talking about? The *decease* of the Messiah in Jerusalem. What does that mean? The Messiah was to fulfill all that was written in the Law and the Prophets concerning himself. His death would be the final destination on earth, and His resurrection would assure even the Old Testament saints the supreme sacrifice for sin had been paid. Wow! What a sight! Jesus standing there with Moses and Elijah. Great biblical events happened on the top of mountains — Mount Sinai, Mount Nebo, Mount Carmel, Mount of Beatitudes, Mount of Transfiguration, and Mount Calvary.

Peter, not fully knowing at this time that Jesus was greater than Moses or Elijah, wanted to build three tabernacles for all three of them. Jesus was not going to vanish out of their sight until He stretched forth His arms on the cruel cross.

As is the case many other times in the Scriptures, a cloud overshadowed them all. A voice came out of the cloud and said, "This is my beloved son: hear him." This is similar to the words spoken from heaven at the baptism of Jesus: "This is my beloved son in whom I am well pleased" (Matt. 3:17). These words were confirming the confession that Peter had made a few days earlier, that Jesus really was God's Son. They were to listen to Him, for they were hearing the very words of God. When the voice ended, they saw Jesus only. They did not tell anyone what had happened. Can we try to imagine what was going through their minds?

The disciples would never forget that night, and Peter mentions it in his writings in 2 Peter 1:16–18, and the apostle John seems to recall this episode in John 1:14 and 1 John 1:1–2. They did not follow fables or what someone else had told them, they followed the One with whom they walked and talked — the One who had allowed them to see Him in His glory.

What does all this mean to us? It tells us that the future is bright and glorious for the believers in Messiah. As we journey through this dark world, what comfort there is in knowing that one day "corruption shall put on incorruption," on that great resurrection day. No wonder the disciples were not afraid to die at the end of their earthly lives — they knew beyond a shadow of a doubt that "to be absent from the body was to be present with the Lord." They had experienced the truth of Isaiah 7:14: "His name shall be called Immanuel, God with us." How beautiful heaven must be, for it holds the perfect Savior of the world. The only way that we will be able to see His glory, is for Him to make us just like himself!

FINAL LESSONS AT GALILEE

Mark 9:14–50
Matthew 17:14–18:35
Luke 9:37–50

After Jesus and the disciples came down from the Mount of Transfiguration, they walked about 30 miles back down to Galilee. On their way, a great multitude was gathered, and a father brought his only son to Jesus with a deaf and dumb spirit. The disciples could not cast the demon out, and Jesus was disturbed with their lack of faith. Jesus told the father, "If thou canst believe, all things are possible to him that believeth." The father began to cry, and *his* words have been *my* words many times: "Lord, I believe; help thou mine unbelief." When Jesus cast the evil spirit out of the boy, he was as a dead man. But Jesus took him by the hand, and lifted him up. The disciples asked, "Why could not we cast him out?" Jesus said, "This kind can come forth by nothing but by prayer and fasting."

Jesus began to tell His disciples about His death, and that the third day He would rise again. These disciples felt sorrowful, because Jesus was their life . . . and He is going to be killed?

According to Exodus 30:13, every male 20 years old and over was to pay a half shekel each year, atonement money, for the upkeep of the temple. Even the poor had to pay this half shekel tribute money. The religious leaders were in Capernaum collecting the tribute money, and they asked Peter, "Doth not your Master pay tribute?" To which he replied, "Yes." And before he got a chance to ask Jesus, Jesus knew his thoughts, and He asked Peter, "Of whom do the kings of the earth take custom or tribute? Of their own children, or of strangers?" Peter said, "Of strangers." Then Jesus said, "Then are the children free."

Which meant that He was the one they were supposed to be honoring back in the temple, but they were not His children. The temple had become filled with money-hungry pretenders. Jesus was the fulfillment of what the temple stood for. He would now live in the people, not in temples of wood and stone. But to keep from offending the people, He told Peter to go fishing. Cast a hook in the sea, and the first fish you catch, you open his mouth, then you will find a piece of money. Take it, and pay both of our taxes. What a miracle!

Next, there were two problems that the disciples had. One, they were arguing who was the greatest, and, two, they had rebuked a man for casting out demons, because he would not join their group. Jesus gave them a lesson that they would never forget.

He took a child in His arms, and said, "Whosoever therefore shall humble himself as this little child, the same shall be the greatest in the kingdom of heaven." The way to be great, is to become small. What did Jesus say in the Sermon on the Mount? "Blessed are the poor in spirit, for theirs is the kingdom of heaven." They would never learn how to serve in God's kingdom, as long as they were jealous of each other.

They must also learn how to receive God's children, and not offend them. A millstone in those days was turned by a donkey, as it crushed the olives in an olive mill. The millstone weighed over a hundred pounds. As Jesus looked at the millstone in Capernaum, and looked out to the sea, which was just a few feet away, He said, "And whosoever shall offend one of these little ones that believe in Me, it is better for him that a millstone were hanged about his neck, and he were cast into the sea." Then He started talking about the fires of hell. With a child in His arms, He talked about hell? Why? Because the most precious thing to Jesus is His children. They must beware how they treat His other children.

He closes this lesson by telling them that they need to have "salt in themselves." They needed to be *well-seasoned* followers. Don't be disputing among yourselves about who is the greatest. Don't turn My children away just because they are not a part of your group. I'm keeping a record of everything My children are doing for Me; even a cup of cold water will not be forgotten.

What a lesson for all of us, in a day when many professing believers have a spirit of competition. If we can help someone else reach God's will for their lives, even if it makes us look smaller, we must do it. Who has the right to say that others have to be a part of *his* church, or *his* denomination? It's all about serving in God's kingdom, and there is a place for all of His children. One good test that we can all take from time to time is, "We know that we have passed from death to life, because we love the brethren."

Jesus told the parable of the lost sheep. Just like a man leaving the 90 and 9 sheep to search for that one lost sheep, and when he finds it, he rejoices, the disciples were to rejoice when someone who is lost is found. If there is joy in heaven when a lost sheep is found, there certainly should be rejoicing on earth among the children of God.

Jesus goes on to say, however, "For where two or three are gathered together in my name, there am I in the midst of them." This verse has been so misrepresented over the years. He was talking about disciplining a child of God when they do something against us. If he or she will repent when we go and talk to them, we have gained a brother or sister. But if they will not hear of it, we take two or three witnesses, and if they still will not hear, we bring it before the church. If they still will not repent, then they can be excommunicated. The previous verse is talking about Jesus being in the midst, when we make those serious decisions concerning another brother.

But just in case the disciples, or we, should become arrogant or self-righteous, Jesus tells them and us to forgive a trespassing brother "until seventy times seven." May we never forget the great debt that was forgiven when we came to the Lord. And if we do not forgive others, our Heavenly Father is not going to hear our prayers when we need forgiveness. God knows and sees our sins, even when others do not see them. Just like Jesus knew what the disciples were thinking before they answered Him, He sees our lives everyday. He is *El Roi*, "the Lord who sees me!"

Galilee, Galilee

Galilee, Galilee,
Where Jesus walked across your hills,
Where His glory lingers still,
Galilee, Galilee,
Where Jesus opened blinded eyes,
Into the darkness came the light,
There's no other place like Galilee.

Galilee, Galilee,
Where Jesus walked the stormy deep
And to the wind He spoke peace.
Galilee, Galilee,
The one the prophets told about
Came to you there is no doubt.
There's no other place like Galilee.

O Galilee how special you are
To be chosen as the place
Where Messiah would come to live.
Your mountains saw His face.

Galilee, Galilee,
Consider how your flowers grow,
They tell the story of long ago.
Galilee, Galilee,
You make the Bible come alive
When I walk your shores at night.
He's real to me in Galilee.
He's real to me in Galilee.

Written by Carroll Roberson. Copyright: Jesus Is Real Music (BMI)

THE JOURNEY TO JERUSALEM AND THE PEREAN MINISTRY

We now reach a part of the Messiah's ministry that is almost impossible to follow chronologically. Once again, that is not the most important thing; our focus is on the person of the Messiah and His wonderful message and mission. We know that Jesus went from Galilee through parts of Samaria, then to Perea ("land beyond Jordan"), on up to Jerusalem, then went back to Perea, before entering Jerusalem the last time (John 10:40–42).

However, for the sake of better understanding the Gospels, we will group the entire Perean ministry together, with a brief stop at Samaria. It is interesting that there are nine chapters in the Gospel of Luke that are not recorded in the other three Gospels.

A Lesson from Samaria

Luke 9:51–56   As the Messiah was leaving Galilee, He and His disciples went through a certain village in Samaria. The people did not receive Jesus very well, because His face was focused on Jerusalem, where He would have to die. Then two of Jesus' disciples, James and John, *Boanerges*, "sons of thunder" (Mark 3:17), wanted to call fire down from heaven and destroy the people. But

The Christ:

listen to what Jesus said, "Ye know not what manner of spirit ye are of. For the son of man is not come to destroy men's lives, but to save them." The disciples were learning how to love *all* people. Jesus used the Samaritans to help teach them that lesson.

If we are filled with the Spirit of the Messiah, we will have no prejudice in our hearts toward anyone. We must remember that the gospel was to the Jews, then to the Gentiles. If it were not for God's wonderful grace, the Gentiles would have never heard the gospel. There is no room in God's kingdom for anti-Semitism or animosity toward any race or individual. I'm reminded once again of that powerful passage in John 3:16–17, "For God so loved the world, that he gave his only begotten Son, that whosoever believeth in him should not perish, but have everlasting life. For God sent not his Son into the world to condemn the world; but that the world through him might be saved."

TEST OF DISCIPLESHIP

Luke 9: 57–62 As Jesus and His disciples journeyed on, a man said unto him, "Lord, I will follow thee whithersoever thou goest." Jesus, knowing the hearts of all men (John 2:25), saw that this man was following for the wrong reason. He thought Jesus would give him health and wealth all of his life. But Jesus turned and said, "Foxes have holes, and birds of the air have nests; but the Son of Man hath not where to lay his head." In other words, "You must follow me for *who* I am, and not for *what* you can get out of me. There may be some times when the world seems to have more than you, but you must keep on following me."

Then Jesus said to another, "Follow me," but he said, "Lord, suffer me first to go and bury my father." There certainly wasn't anything wrong with this man wanting to take care of his deceased father, but Jesus was teaching him a tremendous truth: "Let the dead bury the dead; but go thou and preach the kingdom of God," or rephrased, "Even spiritually dead people can bury the physical dead. You follow Me, and preach the gospel to those who still have time to repent."

Then there was another who said, "Lord, I will follow thee; but let me first go bid them farewell, which are at home at my house." Jesus knew the dangers of going back home, so He told him, "No man, having put his hand to the plough, and looking back, is fit for the kingdom of God." We cannot follow Jesus if we are constantly look-ing back to our past failures or past successes. Too many times, we live in the past, and miss what God has for us in the present. There are many who are saved, who are not *disciples*. Following Jesus is a serious matter, and there has to be a committed life.

So we cannot be disciples of our Lord *if:*

1) We follow Him just for the physical blessings
2) We do not realize a sense of urgency
3) We are always looking back

We cannot let anything stop us from following Yeshua. Maybe we have had bad things done *unto* us, or maybe we have done bad things *to* ourselves. We all have made wrong decisions in life, but once we find the mercies of God, through the Messiah, all of the past is forgiven, and He will forgive our present-day sins, as we confess them to Him. The Lord uses even our mistakes to make us better disciples for the Kingdom, just like He did in the lives of the 12 disciples. Striving to be holy, we lay aside everything that hinders us, and that means even the good things that take up most of our time. The longer I try to follow my Lord, the more I realize how narrow the road really is to heaven!

THE 70 SENT OUT

Luke 10:1–24   As we look back on the Galilean ministry, we find that Jesus had compassion on the multitudes, because He saw them as sheep not having a shepherd. Here we see His compassion again, as He sends forth 70 other disciples to go before Him into the cities and places He was about to enter. The harvest was great, but the laborers were few.

He tells them that they are as "lambs among wolves." They are to travel very light — no money purse, no scrip, no extra shoes, and do not give honor to any man.

Their meals would be provided by the houses that received them. They were to heal their sick, and leave their peace, *shalom,* with them. If the houses did not receive them, they were to wipe the very dust of the city off their feet as a testimony against it (the city). The kingdom of God must be announced that it has come, and they would suffer severe punishment. Even the city of Sodom in the Old Testament, would not suffer as much, because the Messiah was in their very midst.

At this time, Jesus thinks back on the cities of Galilee, where He had walked. He begins to upbraid the cities of Chorazin, Bethsaida, and Capernaum. He said that the Gentile territory of Tyre and Sidon would suffer *less* than them. Today, those Galilean cities are left in rubble, and the Gentile city of Tiberias is still there.

When the people received the disciples, they were receiving Jesus as well. When the 70 returned, they were rejoicing because the evil spirits were subject unto them. But Jesus said, "Rather rejoice, because your names are written in heaven."

Jesus, seeing how His Kingdom was rejected by many of the wise and prudent, and His disciples were just ordinary men, began to rejoice. He thanked the Father for revealing the mysteries of the kingdom to babes, and for hiding them from the wise of the world. Then He turned to His disciples and said, "Blessed are the eyes which see the things that ye see." Many of the Old Testament kings and prophets were not allowed to see the things they saw. What a thought, just to have been one of the disciples who walked with Jesus! When we read the Gospels, we are reading from men who were *eyewitnesses* of the Messiah.

As Jesus did, we too must learn how to rejoice in what God has done through us and through others. It's all about God's kingdom, and pointing others to the Savior. When we see others falling in love with Jesus the Messiah, we should shout, "Hallelujah!" The word comes from *hallelu*, which means "praise," and *yah*, which is part of the Hebrew name for God, *Yahweh*. So may we learn to "PRAISE GOD"!

THE PARABLE OF THE GOOD SAMARITAN

Luke 10:25–37 An expert in the Jewish law came to our Lord, tempting Him, and asked Him a question, "What shall I do to inherit eternal life"? This Jewish lawyer had no concept of guilt; it was the old Judaism of self-righteousness. He thought that eternal life was the *reward* of good works.

Jesus pointed him to the place that he claimed to be so schooled in, the old law, the Torah. Why? Because it is the law that brings people to their sin, and shows them their need of a Savior. So Jesus asked him, "What is written in the law? How readest thou?" The man quoted the verses that are repeated every day by a religious Jew, Deuteronomy 6:4–5, "*Sh'ma, yisra'el! Adonai eloheinu, Adonai echad*" (Hear O Israel; the Lord our God is one Lord) and "Thou shalt love the Lord thy God with all thine heart, and with all thy soul, and with all thy might." The Jewish lawyer began at verse 5, and then added part of Leviticus 19:18, "and thy neighbor as thyself." These two verses contained the relationship between God and man.

Jesus answered him, "Thou hast answered right; this *do*, and thou shalt live." When the man tried to justify himself, and tried to show Jesus that it wasn't so easy to determine who one's neighbor was, Jesus gave a parable to show just how far orthodox Judaism was from the true meaning of God's written Word.

In Luke 10:30–35, Jesus told of a man who was walking from Jerusalem to Jericho, who was beaten and robbed and left half dead. This is about 21 miles of isolated road, noted to be very dangerous. As one travels downward 2,500 feet, the canyons provide a good hideout for robbers. Everyone knew about this road and the common dangers.

Jesus says that a priest saw the man, and passed him by. A Levite passed him by as well. But a half-heathen Samaritan came by and showed compassion on the poor, helpless man. Not only did he pour olive oil and wine on his wounds, but he placed him on his animal, and took him to the nearest lodging. Furthermore, he paid for his stay, and promised to pay the remaining cost, when he came back by.

Then Jesus asked the Jewish lawyer a piercing question, "Which now of these three, thinkest thou, was neighbour unto him that fell among the thieves?" A religious Jew would not even mention the name "Samaritan," so he just said, "He that showed mercy to him." Then Jesus said, "Go, and do thou likewise."

Not only can we see that anyone in need is our neighbor, but this is also a *"gospel parable."* Jesus the Messiah became our neighbor, and paid the utmost cost for our sin-wounded lives. The blood that He shed on the cross provides for us heaven. Can you think of a better place to spend eternity? He sees us on the road of life, wherever we may be. He truly is the fulfillment of the story of the good Samaritan. Yeshua the Messiah will not pass you by!

LORD, TEACH US TO PRAY

Luke 11:1–13 Here we have three sections concerning prayer, and they begin with the disciples seeing and hearing the Messiah pray. Can you try to imagine what it must have been like to have heard Jesus pray? I'm sure we would have said the same thing, "Lord, teach us to pray." John the Baptist taught his disciples how to pray as well. So let's now look briefly at these three sections.

1) *Verses 1–4: The model prayer*
   We see that God is not just a faraway God who is the Creator only. Through faith in Messiah, God is our Heavenly Father. We can go to Him as His children. We should pray for His name to be "hallowed," or glorified. We should pray for His name to not be profaned. It's interesting that the Hebrew language is the only language that does not have a curse word. But the Israelites profaned His name by worshiping other gods, and we must pray for His name to be honored in all that we do. Also, our focus should be on His kingdom — may God's kingdom be enlarged. May God's will be done, not our little wishes. Just ask God for one day's provision at a time. We may not live to see tomorrow, just focus on today. As we pray, we ask for forgiveness of our sins, and we forgive others who have sinned against us. We pray for God to protect us from Satan and temptation. We all should heed this instruction.

2) *Verses 5–10: The parable of the importunate friend*
Jesus said, "If one of you have a friend, and he comes knocking on your door at midnight, asking for three loaves of bread, and he keeps knocking, will you not give him the bread? Although your children are asleep, you will get up because he keeps knocking." Then Jesus said, "Ask, and it shall be given you; seek, and ye shall find; knock, and it shall be opened unto you." Our lesson from this is to keep asking, keep seeking, keep knocking. Do not be discouraged when the answer does not come immediately.

3) *Verses 11–13: The parable of fatherhood*
Using the imagery of fishermen gathering every kind of object from their nets, such as stones from the bottom of the lake, water snakes, or even scorpions that might find a hiding place in a dry net on shore, Jesus gives us a wonderful truth. If one of our children were to ask us for bread, we wouldn't give them a stone. If they were to ask for fish, we wouldn't give them a serpent. If they were to ask for an egg, we wouldn't give them a scorpion. So if we, being evil, give good gifts unto our children, how much more will our Heavenly Father give us? This was a style of rabbinical teaching, called *kalvohomer*, comparing the small with the great (read Matt. 6:24–34).

So as we pray, may we remember these important lessons, and receive the Holy Spirit into our lives each day. God really does *hear* our prayers, because the blood of Yeshua the Messiah has been shed (read Heb. 10:19–20).

Woe unto You, Pharisees

The contest that Jesus had with the Pharisees is woven throughout the Gospels. However, we should never be guilty of thinking that all of the Pharisees were bad; there were some good ones, just like any other religious groups of people. But for the most part, they had fallen into hypocrisy and were following man-made traditions. The Messiah came to rightly establish the law, not misinterpret the law, like the Pharisees did (read Matt. 5:17–20).

Here, I would like to group many passages together for the sake of better understanding. This section we will focus on the *P'rushim*, better known as the Pharisees.

Luke 11:14–28

To summarize this passage, the Pharisees accused the Messiah of casting out demons by the power of Satan. This shows how far off they were from understanding the kingdom of God. Why would Satan cast out Satan? When Jesus cast out demons, it proved that the kingdom of God had come, and that the Son of God was stronger than Satan.

The Jewish establishment was not worshiping false gods during the time of Messiah. They had swept the house, and the outside was clean, but they were in a *worse* condition. They were "hypocrites," and because of their hypocritical system, they rejected the Messiah when He came. The word "hypocrite" in the Greek language is *hypocrites*, which means "actor." Some scholars believe that Jesus sat in the Roman theaters in the nearby cities of Nazareth, Zippori, or Sepphoris, where He borrowed the name "hypocrite." But when you look at the word in Hebrew, it is *chaneph*, which means "soiled with sin, corrupt, defiled, impious." I do not believe Jesus had to borrow from anyone, and I doubt very seriously if He ever attended a Roman theater. The Messiah knew what was going on all around Him, but He grew up in a very religious, Jewish home. The Hebrew language *already* had a word for the hypocrites.

The Pharisees were pretending to be spiritual, when they were really morally corrupt. Anyone that would condemn the Messiah had to be polluted to the core. Their house was swept and garnished with no idolatry, but their house was *empty*, and filled with demons.

Luke 11:37–38

I find it amazing that Jesus never condemned the open sinner; He offered forgiveness to them. But when it came to the Pharisees, He spoke the strongest condemnation. What a lesson for all of us here.

Because of common courtesy, there was a Pharisee who asked Jesus to come and eat with him. Even though people are not right with God, sometimes they are still courteous. But when he saw that Jesus did not wash His hands before he ate, he started that self-righteous, critical, attitude again. And Jesus began to denounce the Pharisees with His strongest statements.

Luke 11:39–44

They cleaned the outside of their lives, but their hearts were full of wickedness. They were strict about the tithe, but left out the most important things, like judgment and the love of God. They loved to be seen in the upper seats of the synagogue, and greetings in the market places, but they were like unmarked graves, that people walked over and fell into.

Luke 11:45–54

Another man, a religious lawyer, asked Jesus if He was condemning his group too. Jesus the Messiah saw the wickedness in their group as well. They were placing heavy religious burdens on people, refusing to help them in any way. Their fathers killed the prophets, but they built sepulchers for them, claiming to be spiritual. Because of their hypocrisy, Jesus said the blood of all the prophets would be required of that generation. Just think, the religious Jewish establishment killed the Old Testament prophets, then they were going to kill the very Son of God. How blinding religion can be. They were not going to enter into God's kingdom, and they were *preventing* others from entering the Kingdom. After Jesus spoke, they starting trying to catch Him in something of which they could accuse Him. The ones who were supposed to be leading the people *to* God, were keeping them *from* God. They were looking for a sign, but the Messiah told them they would only be given one sign, and that was of the prophet Jonah. "As Jonah was three days and three nights in the whale's belly, so shall the Son of man be three days and three nights, in the heart of the earth" (Matt. 12:38–40).

Luke 12:1–2

When a great multitude of people had gathered, Jesus told them, "Beware ye of the leaven of the Pharisees, which is hypocrisy." Everything will one day be revealed; they will not get away with it. Then He gives a warning to his "friends."

Luke 12:3–12

Be careful what you say in the darkness, it shall be brought to the light. Whatever you say in the closet, will be proclaimed upon the housetops. In other words, do not be hypocrites; be the same wherever you are. Don't put your light under a bushel, let your light shine so others can see (Luke 11:33).

Luke 12:4–7

Do not be afraid of the religious people, they can only kill the body. God has the power to cast you into hell for all of eternity. God will take care of you — you don't have to compromise with the unbelievers. If God does not forget the sparrows, He will certainly not forget you. Even the hairs on your head are numbered.

Luke 12:8–9

His friends were to confess Him before men, and not deny Him. Jesus, not being over 33 years of age here, says that He has the power to judge us one day. This proved that He truly was God in the flesh. It all depends on what we do in this life; if we confess the Savior, He will confess us one day. If we deny the Savior on earth, He will deny us one day.

Luke 12:10–12

Jesus was warning them not to commit the unpardonable sin that the Pharisees had done. Do not blaspheme against the Holy Ghost. They would be brought into the synagogues and magistrates, and the Holy Ghost would teach them what to say. Be careful how you treat the blessed Holy Spirit of God. We must keep in mind, the Pharisees' hypocrisy was in the background of these warnings.

Luke 12:54–59

The religious leaders could discern the weather, but they could not discern the time of the Messiah's visitation. Here the Messiah was in their midst, and because of their man-made traditions, and lack of true love for God, they could not even see who He was. They would pay the uttermost for their unbelief. The face of the sky they could read, but they couldn't see God in the face of Yeshua the Messiah.

One final word about the Pharisees — we still have their kind with us today, people who are blinded by their own interpretations of the Scriptures. People need to do what Jesus told the Pharisees to do in John 5:39: "Search the scriptures." There are so many truths in the Bible that have been hidden for centuries because of people following what someone else said, or following their denomination. We must *heed* the warning here that no matter how spiritual someone appears to be on the outside, the Lord looks on the inside (1 Sam. 16:7).

PARABLE OF THE RICH FOOL

Luke 12:13–34 We are very grateful for our Lord's travels through the "land beyond Jordan." This Perean ministry continues to hold truths that we all need in our own lives. The people were blessed to have the Messiah's presence, and we are blessed to be able to read it today, two thousand years later.

This parable of the rich fool was brought on by a man who asked Jesus a question. "Master, speak to my brother, that he divide the inheritance with me." Jesus let him know that He had not come to earth to divide inheritance money. Jesus knew this man had a covetous problem, so He made this statement, "Take heed, and beware of covetousness; for a man's life consisteth not in the abundance of the things which he possesseth." Then He gave the parable.

There wasn't anything wrong with the man having a good crop, for God allowed him to have an abundant crop. The problem was in Luke 12:18–19: "This will I do; I will pull down *my* barns, and build greater; and there will I bestow all *my* fruits and *my* goods. And I will say to *my* soul, Soul, thou hast much goods laid up for many years; take thine ease, eat, drink, and be merry." Do you see the problem? This man thought it was all his, and he took life for granted. No thanks or gratitude to God, no concern for others — he was wrapped up all within himself.

But God said to him, "Thou fool, this night thy soul shall be required of thee; then whose shall those things be, which thou hast provided?" When God called an end to his earthly life, the man had forgotten about his soul. It was too late!

The main lesson is, "So is he that layeth up treasure for himself, and is not rich toward God." It matters not how many cows we have, or how big our house is, or how much money we have saved. What matters is, do we know the Lord Jesus Christ, and have we served Him faithfully?

Luke 12:22–34

Jesus then turns to His disciples and gives them a repeat of the Sermon on the Mount that He gave back in Galilee. Using the Hebraic style of teaching again called *kalvohomer*, He says, "If God takes care of the flowers and the birds, how much more will he take care of you?" Yeshua tells them that the world seeks after earthly needs, but your Heavenly Father will provide for you. If we place God's kingdom first, then all of the other things will be added. "Fear not little flock; for it is your Father's good pleasure to give you the kingdom." What a tender statement from our Lord — they were but a *"little flock,"* but He was their Shepherd. The Father delights in giving His

children the kingdom. Jesus goes on to tell them to sell what they have, give alms, and lay their treasures in heaven, and that's where their heart would be.

As we look back in the old Hebrew Scriptures, we find that riches were always a danger. Listen to Deuteronomy 6:10–12: "And it shall be, when the LORD thy God shall have brought thee into the land which he sware unto thy fathers, to Abraham, to Isaac, and to Jacob, to give thee great and goodly cities, which thou buildest not, And houses full of good things, which thou filledst not, and wells digged, which thou diggedst not, vineyards and olive trees, which thou plant-edst not; when thou shalt have eaten and be full; Then beware lest thou forget the LORD, which brought thee forth out of the land of Egypt, from the house of bondage." If the Israelites were to beware of their simple houses, and having fruit and water, *how much more* must we beware of all of the materialism in our modern-day world. The Israelites did forget the Lord, and went after false gods who promised better crops.

The Messiah knew that money, materialism, and prosperity, were going to be a problem, and that's why almost three hundred verses are in the Gospels concerning riches. Jesus was trying to keep His disciples from being sidetracked on their spiritual journey. And He will confront this matter again very soon, as we will see.

If the rich man in the parable had given God the glory and praise for what he was enjoying, God would have probably given him even more. But as is the case normally, when we begin to prosper, we turn our attention on ourselves and our desires. This parable throws up a red flag for all of us!

A GOOD AND
FAITHFUL SERVANT

Luke 12:35–48 Yeshua, the Messiah, gives two connecting parables concerning a faithful servant, *eved* in Hebrew, which means "bond servant." The Old Testament gives us the law of a Hebrew slave in Exodus 21:1–11. After serving his master for six years, the seventh year he could go free. But if the servant loved his master, and wanted to stay with him, the master would drive an awl through the servant's ear. This would mark the servant for life. Our lives should bear the marks of the Lord Jesus.

When a person is a servant of the Lord Jesus Christ, he is bound to Him regardless of circumstances. He serves without wanting recognition, and he is faithful in what God has called him to do.

The first parable concerns the second coming of the Christ. The lesson is, we are to be watchful, and live every day as if it were the last. Jesus will speak about His second coming again in Jerusalem, but here He is giving a warning to the people in the land of Perea, as well as His disciples. The two main verses of this parable are Luke 12:35 and 40, "Let your loins be girded about, and your lights burning. . . . Be ye therefore ready also: for the Son of man cometh at an hour when ye think not." So the first parable warns us all to stay *ready* for the Second Coming.

The next parable deals with being a faithful servant. We can do our own will, or the father's will. Once we have been instructed what to do, we will be held accountable for what we know. If we are faithful in the little things, then one day He will make us rulers over many things. It's interesting that the degree of punishment one day will depend on how much one knows and understands. "And that servant, which knew his lord's will, and prepared not himself, neither did according to his will, shall be beaten with many stripes. But he that knew not, and did commit things worthy of stripes, shall be beaten with few stripes. For unto whomsoever much is given, of him shall much be required: and to whom men have committed much, of him they will ask the more" (Luke 12:47–48).

What a tremendous responsibility we have, once we have heard the gospel of Christ, and have sat under the Word of God for many years. Judgment will be severe for the average church member, who has been given much light. Life is an opportunity to share the wonderful message of Jesus the Messiah. So many things in our lives are important, but they will not count at the Day of Judgment. It's wonderful to have a good marriage, a good family, a nice home, and a long life on earth. But what good are those things, if we miss the real meaning of life? So many Westerners think the Spirit-filled life is all about earthly happiness. The Savior is trying to get us to see what will really matter in the end. We may not have the ability of some, but we *will* be responsible for what we *can* do. Not only serving Christ will count when He returns, but it is the only way to find true happiness. We must be *ready*, and we must be *faithful*. That's the message of the two parables.

MESSIAH, THE
GREAT DIVIDER?

Luke 12:49–53
Luke 14:25–35

One of the great problems we have with professing believers, is that many have the wrong understanding of what it means to follow the Messiah. For example, some think that following Jesus means they will have an easier life, that all of their family and friends will love them and support them. Jesus touched on this in the parable of the sower (Matt. 13:20–21). I have found over the years that many start out following Jesus, and later they are nowhere to be found. Maybe their church confused them, or maybe their families discouraged them, or maybe they just had the wrong idea of what being a Christian involves. Well, in these few verses we have a truth that is seldom mentioned in the modern-day Church.

Luke 12:49–53

Jesus said He had come to send "fire" on the earth. You mean Jesus did not come to bring peace? Of course He did, but He knew that most of the hearers would not come to Him. When a person did decide to make the Messiah their Lord, He knew they would encounter tremendous difficulties, even in their own families. The "baptism" that Jesus is referring to here is not water baptism, but *his death*. If we recall earlier, I mentioned that baptism was a sign of identification, and, in this case, the Word is referring to the death of the Messiah.

The cross of Jesus would bring division in the world. It would even divide families: father against son, son against father, mother against daughter, daughter against mother, mother-in-law against daughter-in-law, and daughter-in-law against mother-in-law (Luke 12:53).

This all ties in with what Jesus asked in Matthew 12:48: "Who is my mother? And who are my brethren?" Not the members of His earthly family, but the ones who did the will of the Father in heaven. Our real family is the family of God. We can see this truth brought out again in Mark 6:4: "A prophet is not without honour, but in his own country, and among his own kin, and in his own house" I have found in my own life that when you are following the true Messiah, Jesus Christ, your own family and your home town can be a big disappointment. When I received Christ over 20 years ago, the first problem I had was my home church, and my immediate family. They had different thoughts of what I was supposed to be, and when I surrendered to Jesus, they were not spiritual enough at the time to accept it. The church was too traditional to understand, and my family was too carnal to understand. I wanted my life to be used in God's kingdom, they wanted me to be big in the eyes of the world. Thank God, through the years, some of them have been touched by the Lord, and they see more clearly now.

If a new convert comes to me, I always tell them the seriousness of living for Jesus Christ. If they are not willing to pay the price, then I do not insist on them joining the Church and having a false sense of security. Until we are ready to pay the cost, we will never pass the test. This is further stated in the next passage.

Luke 14:25–35

Jesus was not elated that a multitude of people were following Him here. He knew the great price they would have to pay if they wanted to be His disciples. So He takes this opportunity to give them a very hard saying: "If any man come to me, and hate not his father, and mother, and wife, and children, and brethren, and sisters, yea, and his own life also, he cannot be my disciple." At first it sounds as though Jesus is asking us to *"hate,"* as we think in English. But the word in this passage for "hate" is *miseo*, which means "to love less." So the Messiah is telling us that we must love Him first and foremost. The meaning of the verse is that we must make Christ top priority in our lives. The cost is high, there must be a cross to carry, and every disciple has his or her *own* cross. This means that a disciple of the Messiah must be willing to suffer for His name's sake. It's not the little health problems we have, or the ordinary, earthly problems we face in our lives. Taking up the cross means to suffer being talked about, being rejected, turned away, and in some cases, completely cut off from our family and friends. When a religious Jew comes to faith in the Jewish Messiah, *Yeshua*, their family disowns them. This is a good example of taking up the cross.

Jesus went on to give three parables about discipleship:

1) *Luke 14:28–30, the parable of the tower:* How sad that someone would start to build a tower, which was common is Jesus' time, and not have enough material or money to finish it. Many people have left their lives like an *unfinished* tower.

2) *Luke 14:31–33, the parable of the king going to war:* In the time of Jesus, war was a very common thing. If a king had 10,000 soldiers, he needed to think long and hard before going against another army that had 20,000. If he didn't sit down first and think it through, he would end up *surrendering* to the larger army when he sees them approaching. Jesus is just giving us the seriousness of following Him. The kingdom of darkness is warring against the kingdom of God. If we are not ready to fight in God's army, and if we do not know who the Messiah is, we will surrender one day to the adversary, Satan. But we must remember, when we are in God's army, we are on the winning side.

3) *Luke 14:34–35, the parable of the savorless salt:* Jesus touched on this back in Galilee, but He wants the new audience of Perea to hear as well. A good disciple must be *well seasoned*. There is no room for a jealous spirit, or a spirit of competition. When someone loses their seasoning, they are good for nothing in the kingdom. I wonder how many believers in Jesus have lost their seasoning? We have *countless* people who say they belong to our Lord, but we have *few* disciples.

It's very easy to get into a comfort zone and think we are serving the Messiah. It's easy to be around nice people, attend air-conditioned church buildings, and live in luxury. It's easy to say, "The Lord is good," when all or our circumstances are good. But what about the bad times? What about when the church is not going so well, our husbands and wives abandon us, or our children refuse to follow Jesus? What about the work place? Do we crawl into a hole when we are persecuted for our faith? Can we stand the testing? There is one way we can — by knowing Jesus as the Messiah, that He died and rose again, that He lives inside of us through the Holy Spirit, by staying in His Word each day, by being grounded in the deeper things of God, by not trusting in our friends (Micah 7:5) or our family. All of our trust must be in the Lord. The more we learn about Him, the more He will fill us with the power to live for Him. It's not "trying to live for the Lord," it is "being filled with the Lord" that stands the testing of life.

The Christ:

Do not Judge
— Repent

Luke 13:1–5   This, again, is a passage that is only found in the Gospel of Luke. Jesus is in the land of Perea, and here we are told of two tragedies that happened in Jerusalem. One is told *to* Jesus, and one is told *by* Jesus.

Tragedy number one is when Pontius Pilate murdered some Galileans, who had come to Jerusalem to worship. The Roman procurator mingled their blood with the blood of their sacrifices. Instead of the Messiah acting startled about the tragedy, He told them something very different than what they were expecting to hear. "Suppose ye that these Galilaeans were sinners above all the Galilaeans, because they suffered such things? I tell you, Nay: but, except ye repent, ye shall all likewise perish."

This was a warning to the people about the Romans, who came in A.D. 70 and destroyed Jerusalem. What Pontius Pilate did was just a sample of what was to come. Instead of these people judging the Galilaeans by thinking they were paying for their sins, these people better repent while they have time.

Then Jesus mentions another tragedy that happened when the tower of Siloam fell on 18 people, and killed them. Listen to what Jesus said again, "Think ye that they were sinners above all men that dwelt in Jerusalem? I tell you, Nay: but, except ye repent, ye shall all likewise perish."

So what does all this mean to us? We should be very careful when something bad happens to people, and not think they were paying for something bad they had done. It's a very common practice for us to pass judgment on others, like they did on the man born blind in

John 9. Sometimes we do suffer for our sins in this life, but that is not the case every time. The Scriptures tell us that even wicked people may prosper, and the righteous may suffer (Ps. 73, 34:19). Life is not always fair, and anything can happen to us, even if we are saved. We should take advantage of every tragedy, and see it as a need for us to repent of our sins. "Boast not thyself of to morrow, for thou knowest not what a day may bring forth" (Prov. 27:1). Just because we are saved, does not mean that we are always protected from tragedy.

The real message from Jesus here is a message of repentance. "Repent," in Hebrew, is *nacham*. The meaning is "to sigh deeply" or "repent within one's self." It means to be so sorry for our sins, that we turn from our sins, and turn to the cross of Jesus. We must change our minds about who we are, about who God is, and what life is all about.

There is something much worse than a earthly tragedy that can happen to us. If we die in our sins and do not see our need for salvation, we will perish forever. What right do we have to judge others, when we are not right with God ourselves? We all need to be reminded that this life is temporary and that eternity never ends!

The Christ:

THE PARABLE OF THE FIG TREE

Luke 13:6–9
Matthew 21:18–22

We will group these two passages together, since they both deal with the parable of the "fig tree," or *te'enah* in Hebrew. The fig tree was a very common fruit tree in the land of Israel, and is used often in parables. Compare the similar Old Testament parable of the vineyard in Isaiah 5:1–7.

In Luke's' passage, a man came looking for figs, but found none. He told the dresser of the vineyard to cut it down. But the dresser said, "Lord, let it alone this year also, till I shall dig about it, and dung it, and if it bear fruit, well: and if not, then after that thou shalt cut it down."

What is the meaning of this parable? Jesus came to His own people looking for spiritual fruit and found none. For *three years*, He walked in the land, performing miracles, preaching and teaching in their streets. After *three years*, He would be crucified, and the third day rise again. He was patient and merciful to Israel, but they rejected their Messiah, and they would be cut down by the Romans in A.D. 70.

The next passage, in Matthew 21:18–22, shows the Messiah placing a curse on a fig tree because it had only leaves and no fruit. The religious establishment had only the religious "leaves of profession" — they did not possess the power of God. That generation would perish, because they were not bearing fruit of God.

Many scholars have tried to use this passage to teach that God is through with Israel. It is here that I would like to say that *"replacement theology"* has done so much damage to Christianity and to our churches. Many of the famous reformers like Luther, Calvin, and others, taught this erroneous doctrine. It teaches that all of the verses pertaining to Israel have been replaced by the Church. In other words, a *"spiritual Israel."* I challenge anyone to read Romans 11, and tell me if God is through with His chosen people. We must rightly divide the Word of truth, and see that some verses are talking about the Church, and some are talking about Israel. The Bible is basically a Jewish book, and the Gentiles have been included in the plan. But it all started with the Jews, and it will end with the Jews. We are living in the "times of the Gentiles," and one day soon, God will close the door for the Gentiles, and deal with His people again. This does not mean that *all* of the Jews will be saved, but the ones who are alive when the Messiah returns will acknowledge their sins and receive Him as their Messiah. One of the true signs that we are approaching the end of the world is that over five million Jews are back in the land of Israel today. This is a direct prophecy — God will bring His people back to Israel, to usher in the Messiah. Now, the Jews are not keeping the Messiah from returning, He will come when the Father tells Him to come. Why didn't they come back to the land a hundred years ago? Why now? We are living in a very exciting day, when we could see the return of the King of kings and Lord of lords. The fact that Israel is hated by most of the world shows that the Battle of Armageddon is drawing closer. America is the best friend Israel has, and we *better* stay that way.

Jesus was a Jew, and when He returns He will be a Jew. When I travel to the Holy Land, an awesome feeling comes over me, because I know that one day the Messianic kingdom will be set up, and I will be there with my Jewish Messiah for 1,000 years, then I will spend eternity with Him!

Yeshua places a curse on the fig tree, not to say that He was through with Israel, but to show the disciples that destruction was coming to that generation. He closed by telling the disciples that if they have enough faith, they can move mountains into the sea. There would be many mountains in the lives of the disciples, and their faith would be the answer. One of the big mountains in their ministry would be the old Jewish religious system that only had the "leaves of religion."

DID JESUS BREAK THE SABBATH?

Luke 13:10–17, Luke 14:1–6
Mark 2:23–28, Mark 3:2–4
Luke 6:1–9, John 5:9–18
John 9:14–16

In Hebrew it is called *Shabbat*. This day of rest in the Bible was Saturday. When we take our tours to Israel, many of the religious Jews still keep the *Shabbat*. It was given by God to the children of Israel as a day of resting from their labors, and acknowledging His goodness. But during the time of Messiah Jesus, this day had turned into a legalistic, cold, burdensome tradition, with no real honor for God.

Yeshua deliberately healed many people on the Sabbath day, to prove to the religious people that they had misunderstood what the true meaning of the Sabbath was all about. Many times Jesus would say to them, "Which of you shall have an ass or an ox fallen into a pit, and will not straightway pull him out on the Sabbath day?" The religious leaders would pull an ox out of the ditch on the Sabbath day, and then condemn the Son of God for pulling a person out of sin on the Sabbath day. It hurt Jesus so much to see people suffering, and suffering came into the world through sin. These religious leaders were committing the worse kind of sin, by placing these suffering people under bondage with their strict observances.

So what does all of this mean to us today? There are many today in our world who still hold to the Sabbath day being on Saturday. There is certainly nothing wrong with this, but here is the problem. When we begin to make others feel guilty because they do not worship on Saturday, then we have fallen back into legalism. Whatever *day* people choose to gather together and worship God is not the important thing, it is *who* we are worshiping. Let me read you something from Paul's letter to the Colossians: "Let no man therefore judge you in meat, or in drink, or in respect of an holy day, or of the new moon, of the *Sabbath* days, *which are a shadow of things to come: but the body is of Christ.*" Notice what Paul said — the Sabbath day was a shadow of things to come. The Messiah fulfilled the old law, *He* is our rest (Heb. 4:9–11), and there is coming a day when the *earth* will be at rest in the Messianic kingdom.

The believers in the early church met on Sunday, the first day of the week (Acts 20:7). This was the day of the resurrection of the Messiah, "the Lord's day." When anyone tries to *make* a Gentile worship on a Jewish *Shabbat,* this is a grave error. There is always the danger of getting lost in a *day*, or a *service,* or a *church*, or *baptism*, or any *external ritual,* and losing sight of Yeshua the Messiah!

Once again, I want to repeat myself to make things clear. If you want to worship on Saturday, that is wonderful, but just make sure you are worshiping the true and living God, in spirit and in truth! No one should condemn you for that, and you should *not* condemn anyone else for *not* worshiping on that day. Legalism is a subtle but dangerous trap to fall into. We, too, can become like the Pharisees of old, and miss the One who came to give us true rest!

STRIVE TO ENTER
THE STRAIT GATE

Luke 13:22–33   As Jesus was going through the cities and villages, teaching on His way to Jerusalem, someone said to Him, "Lord, are there few that be saved?" And Jesus said to him, "Strive to enter in at the strait gate: for many, I say unto you, will seek to enter in, and shall not be able." What was Jesus saying? There would come a day when many of the Jewish people who saw the Messiah while He was on earth, would try to bargain with the Lord and say, "We have eaten and drunk in thy presence, and thou hast taught in our streets." But the Lord will say, "I tell you, I know you not whence ye are; depart from me, all ye workers of iniquity. There shall be weeping and gnashing of teeth, when ye shall see Abraham, and Isaac, and Jacob, and all the prophets, in the kingdom of God, and you yourselves thrust out."

Just because Jesus had been in their presence, did not mean they would be saved. They were to strive now! What a sad thought, to be able to see the Old Testament saints in the Kingdom, and to be thrust out. While Jesus was speaking, some of the Pharisees came to Him and said, "Get thee out, and depart hence: for Herod will kill thee." This shows that Jesus was in the land of Perea, which was governed by Herod Antipas. Jesus wasn't worried about Herod, He knew that he would be used to fulfill the Hebrew Scriptures. The Messiah must die, and Herod would be one of those in the plan. Jesus wanted the Pharisees to know that He would be killed, and after three days He would rise again. Jesus said it was unthinkable that a prophet should perish out of anywhere other than Jerusalem.

What a warning this is for us today. Just because we attend a place called "church" and have seen the Lord touch others, does not assure us that we will be saved in the end. We must strive to enter the gate ourselves. This thought was preached by Jesus back in Galilee, in the Sermon on the Mount. He talked about the strait gate, and the narrow way, and how *few* would enter (Matt. 7:13–14). It's not automatic because we were raised in a Christian home, or because we believe and do Christian things, or because we give mental accent to the gospel. The doctrine of Calvinism is definitely wrong when it says that some were elected for heaven and some were elected for hell. The responsibility is given to all of us to repent and believe. There is a big little word in the bible — "if." *If* we believe that Jesus of Nazareth is the Messiah, *if* we believe He died and rose again, *if* we confess Him with our mouth and with our lives, then we shall be saved. No one will be able to blame God if they do not make it to heaven. Salvation is a finished work of the Messiah, and we must humble ourselves and accept Him as our personal Savior. The gate is strait and narrow, only one person at a time.

So many people I have seen in the churches where I have preached made a decision years ago, and did not know what they were doing. Maybe they joined a church when they were young, because others joined the church. Maybe they said a prayer with a preacher and did not fully understand what biblical salvation was all about. Maybe, over the years, they have grown so cold on God, they do not know anymore if they were really saved. I do not believe there are as many people who have been truly born again as most people think.

The thing to do is to go to God in earnest prayer, and tell Him that you believe in Jesus, the Son of God. That you believe and trust Him for your eternal salvation, that He is the Messiah, who died for your sins, and rose again the third day. Then follow through with your decision, and get involved in a Bible-believing congregation, follow the Lord in water baptism, and start studying the Scriptures daily. Share your faith with those around you, and *strive* to live a holy and godly life.

Spiritual Lessons about Weddings and Suppers

Luke 14:7–11   **W**hen Jesus saw how the Pharisees loved the praise of men, He gave three parables back to back. We shall begin with the parable of the wedding feast.

"When thou art bidden of any man to a wedding, sit not down in the highest room. . . . But . . . sit down in the lowest room." Weddings in the time of Jesus were very festive, and lasted for a week. These Pharisees wanted people to go away and spread the news that they had the highest seat in the wedding. It was a very humbling thing for someone to be asked to get up and let someone else have their seat.

We must not desire the praise of others, but just serve God in humility, and if He wants to move us up to a higher place, then that is His decision. Many people today who hold positions in the modern Church, cover up their lack of spirituality by having a title or sitting in a place of authority. The spirit of the Pharisees is still with us today.

Luke 14:12–15

This is a parable woven in between the other two parables. We should not invite people over to our homes, hoping to be rewarded later. It's easy to invite relatives, or rich neighbors, who we know are going to be good to us in return. We should help those who cannot pay us back — this is pleasing to our Lord. When one lives a life of true humility, he does not seek the praise of men, and he gives to others, expecting nothing in return. Our service to the Messiah must be from a pure heart, or it will not count at the Day of Judgment.

Luke 14:16–24

This is the parable of the great supper. When a certain man invited his servants to come to supper, they began to make excuses. One said he had just bought a piece of land; one said he had just purchased five yoke of oxen, and one said he had just gotten married. All of them asked to be excused from the great supper. The master became very angry, and told his servant to go out *quickly* into the streets and lanes of the city, and bring in the poor, the maimed, the halt, and the blind. The servant did what his master said, but there was still more room available. Then the servant was told to go out into the highways and hedges, and compel others to come to the supper. The Master's house *would* be filled.

The Pharisees had been invited, but refused the Messiah's offer. Others would receive the invitation — the outcasts of society and eventually, the Gentiles. The great supper would be filled with people after all.

When we read the Gospels, it is very clear that the Messiah showed special love and mercy to the ones the Pharisees despised. While the Pharisees were pretending to be the children of God, God was making other people His children, who were the humble ones. If we exalt ourselves, we shall be brought down, but if we humble ourselves, God will lift us up.

I am so thankful that the Lord has given us the invitation to come to His supper. What a day that will be, when we gather around the table with the Lord himself, for that great supper in heaven!

A Lost Sheep, a Lost
Coin, and a Lost Son

Luke 15   One of the best ways to understand any passage of Scripture is to study the background of the text. Here it is very helpful to read the first few words of Luke 15. "Then drew near unto him all the publicans and sinners for to hear him. And the Pharisees and scribes murmured, saying, This man receiveth sinners, and eateth with them."

The poor Pharisee, while judging Jesus and judging others, could not see his need for forgiveness. None are so blind as the religious people. We can see a perfect picture of this, when we read Luke 18:9–14, the parable of the Pharisee and the publican.

The Pharisees wore phylacteries (little boxes containing Scriptures around their foreheads and wrists), they fasted, they tithed, they enlarged the borders of their garments in order to look more spiritual. They loved to be called "rabbi" (Matt. 23:1–12). A large portion of the teachings of the Messiah was given with the Pharisees in mind.

We now come to one of the most familiar chapters in the Gospels — three parables that have a tremendous lesson for all of us. We must not fall into the trap of trying to build doctrine or teach theology from a parable. They are given to illustrate a principle, and we must see the overall truth that the Messiah is teaching us. Let's look at these three individually.

Luke 15:3–7, The parable of the lost sheep: Tending to sheep was the number one occupation among the poor. When 1 sheep was lost, it was certainly worth going after. The Gospel of Matthew tells us the man went searching through the mountains. The Hebrew word for sheep is *tse'own*, which means "to migrate." Especially in southern Israel, the shepherds have to guide their sheep to the grassy hillsides, where the dew is greater. The northern slopes stay shady the longest, and this is where they find grass for the sheep. The sheep have the tendency to go astray and get lost in the deserted mountains. If not found, they will die, so the shepherd goes in search of his lost sheep. Even though he has 90 and 9 safe in the fold, that 1 sheep is valuable. When he finds the little lost sheep, he lays it on his shoulders, rejoicing, and brings it back home. Then he calls his friends and neighbors to rejoice with him, for he has found the lost sheep. Jesus said, "I say unto you, that likewise joy shall be in heaven over one sinner that repenteth, more than over ninety and nine just persons, which need no repentance."

The self-righteous scribes and Pharisees should have been rejoicing because the lost sinners and publicans were getting saved, but they were complaining about Jesus taking up time with them. They felt as though they needed no repentance. One soul causes all

of heaven to rejoice. We should always rejoice when a lost sheep is found, no matter what their past has been. One of the most precious pictures in my mind is to think of Jesus holding me in His arms, just like a little sheep. "I once was lost, but now I'm found, I was blind, but now I see."

Luke 15:8–10, The parable of the lost coin: There was no paper money in the time of Jesus, only coins. All of the houses where the common people lived had either dirt flooring or cobbled stone flooring. It was very common for a coin to be lost in the crevices of the rocks. When this poor woman lost a coin, she took a lighted olive oil lamp (there were no candles in those days) and swept the entire house. That coin was so valuable to her that, when she found it, she called all of her neighbors and friends together to rejoice with her. The Messiah points out that all of the angels in heaven rejoice, when one sinner is found. These Pharisees had no love for the lost, and saw no need to rejoice.

Luke 15:11–32, The parable of the lost son: This is probably one of the most commonly used passages in preacher preparation over the years. The story is told of a man who had two sons. The younger son committed a grave sin by asking his father for his inheritance. (This was not to be done before the father died, so this young man would have been cast out of the Jewish community.) The father gave him his inheritance, and the younger son went into a far country and wasted his inheritance. We know it was a Gentile country, because he was feeding the pigs. While feeding the pigs, the younger son came to himself and he realized that even the servants back at his father's house had more than he did. He decided to go back home, and maybe his father would just make him a hired servant, since he was no longer worthy to be his son. He rehearsed what he would say to his father, but something happened as he approached the little community. The father saw him from a distance, and ran, and fell on his neck and kissed him. This younger son was saved all of the embarrassment that he would have received from the Jewish community. While the son was telling his father how unworthy he was to be called his son, the father started preparing a great celebration. The younger son was given the best robe, a ring, and shoes on his feet. A fatted calf was even killed, and they made a feast. The father said, "For this my son was dead, and is alive again; he was lost, and is found."

But we must not miss the rest of the story. The older brother, who had been working in the field, was walking back home when he heard the music and dancing that was going on. He asked one of the hired servants what all of this was about. The hired servant told him about his younger brother who had come home, and they had killed the fatted calf to celebrate. The older brother became very angry, and would take no part in the celebration. Listen to what the older son told his father: "Lo, these many years do I serve thee, neither transgressed I at any time thy commandment; and yet thou never gavest me a kid, that I might make merry with my friends, but as soon as this thy son was come, which hath devoured thy living with harlots, thou hast killed him the fatted calf."

We can see the self-righteousness of the Pharisees in Luke 15:2, 7, and 29–30. The Pharisees were *murmuring* about Jesus eating with the sinners. The Pharisees thought they *needed no repentance*, and they were *like the older son* who was jealous of his younger brother, and felt as though his younger brother had been too sinful for the father to make a party for his homecoming.

The main lesson in these parables is to see the great love of God, that *searches* for the lost. The *rejoicing* that occurs when someone is found. And how the *heart of God* feels when one of His lost children is found. Do we rejoice when others are saved? Are we jealous when someone receives attention, and we do not? The Pharisees needed the love of God in their hearts, and God was standing in their midst, and they missed Him!

THE DANGER OF RICHES

Luke 16
Luke 18:18–27

One of the big problems that the modern-day health-and-wealth preachers have is that the Messiah lived among the poor, and He lived a very simple lifestyle. Like the Jews of old, many think a sign of spirituality is prosperity. If a follower of the Messiah is supposed to always be healthy and wealthy, then Jesus of Nazareth was a failure. And even though being poor doesn't make anyone more godly, and wealth can be used for God's kingdom, we, nevertheless, have a warning from our Lord concerning the danger of riches, or "unrighteous mammon." Almost three hundred verses in the gospels warn us about riches, and we, in our materialistic, Western world, seem to ignore what Jesus was saying. I would like to briefly look at the 16th chapter of Luke's Gospel, and then the familiar story of the rich young ruler in Luke 18.

Luke 16:1–13

Jesus gave the parable of the unjust steward to show us that, even though the steward was unjust in what he did, he was wise. He knew he was going to be fired by the rich man for wasting his goods, so he quickly went to the rich man's debtors and reduced what they owed. This assured him that he would have a place to stay after he was released from his duties. Jesus used this parable to teach us that sometimes even lost people are wiser than saved people, when it comes to using money. We are to use the "unrighteous mammon," to make friends with it, that we will meet in heaven one day. The main verse is verse 11: "If therefore ye have not been faithful in the unrighteous mammon, who will commit to your trust the true riches?" The key is "true riches." Having money is not the "true riches"; it's having Christ in our hearts, and using what we have for His glory. If we cannot use a temporary thing like money for God's kingdom, then why would He entrust to us the "true riches"? We must be faithful in the little things first, before God will give us the great mysteries of His Kingdom. Jesus closes this parable by repeating something He had said back in the Sermon on the Mount. "No servant can serve two masters; for either he will hate the one, and love the other; or else he will hold to the one, and despise the other. Ye cannot serve God and mammon."

Luke 16:19–31

The story of the rich man and Lazarus, *El'azar,* is a very frequently used passage, but we must not get lost in this story and try to teach theology. Jesus is trying to give us a lesson here. The main lesson is, if the rich man had used his "unrighteous mammon" to help the poor, old Lazarus, he would have not ended up in hell fire. He didn't have enough of God's light inside of him to care about the poor and needy. When their lives ended on earth, Lazarus was in the joy of the Lord, and the rich man was in torment. The sad thing is that the rich man could remember in hell how he treated Lazarus. To be in hell, tossing and tumbling in a bottomless pit, forever and ever, and then being able to remember what one should have done is a horrifying thought indeed. This story proves again, that sometimes the godly person may have little in this life, but will enjoy heaven in the end.

Luke 18:18-27

I have heard the story of the rich young ruler misinterpreted many times over the years. Saying that God wants every one of His children to sell what they have and give to the poor, but that is not the message here. This young man was a religious Jew, who believed strongly in the law of Moses. He had lived a very clean life, and he thought he was on his way to eternal life. He didn't know that he was committing idolatry. Jesus set him up to show him what his hindrance was. The man thought he was living by the commandments morally, but he loved his money too much to enter heaven. His god was money, not the God of Israel. When Jesus told him to sell everything, and give it to the poor, he walked away sorrowfully. The Bible says he was *very rich*. The Hebrew word for rich is *chayil*, which means "substance," "army," or "wealth" (in this case, "wealth"). Jesus didn't say this to most people, but He knew what this man's problem was. He used this man to show the disciples the danger of riches.

Listen to these important verses: "And when Jesus saw that he was very sorrowful, he said, how hardly shall they that have riches enter into the kingdom of God! For it is easier for a camel to go through a needle's eye, than for a rich man to enter into the kingdom of God. And they that heard it said, who then can be saved? [thinking that wealth was a sign of salvation] And He said, the things which are impossible with men, are possible with God."

So many theologians and Bible scholars have tried to explain away the seriousness of the Messiah's teaching here. Some have said that the "eye of the needle" was a gate in Jerusalem, where the camels had to stoop way down before they could enter, meaning that rich people have to humble themselves to be saved. But when you study the style of teaching during the time of the Messiah, this was a "hyperbole," an extreme way of teaching, in order to get people's attention. Jesus was talking about a *real* camel, and a *real* sewing needle. The point was made by the disciples, "How then can they be saved?" They knew it was impossible for a camel to go through the eye of a sewing needle, and it was commonly thought that the poor were outside of God's blessings. But Jesus said, with God all things are possible. Salvation is not possible with man, only through the miracle of God's saving grace.

Rich men can be saved, but it is very difficult. Until we abandon everything, and see our need of the blood of Jesus Christ, we will not be truly born again. So many people are like this rich, young ruler, who live a clean moral life, but they are lovers of money. Attending church and doing religious deeds will not save anyone. Can't you just hear people saying today, "Well, the Lord sure has blessed me, I must be doing something right." Worldly riches don't prove anything in God's eyes. Some see life as an opportunity to use their talents for God, but most people see money as a thing to trust, a goal within itself.

I'm reminded of a little story I heard long ago of a man who passed away in a little community. Two men were talking in a country store about his passing, and one man said, "Did you hear about Josh? He passed away the other day. I wonder how much money he left?" To which the other man replied, "He left it all!"

DIVORCE — WHAT DOES THE BIBLE REALLY SAY?

Matthew 19:3–12 Very few subjects have been misrepresented in the Church as much as the subject of divorce. Because of many traditional beliefs, and trying to build a teaching based on a translation of the Bible, many have been confused and have wrestled with this issue. But we must search the Scriptures to find the real answer as always, and understanding a little more about the Jewish culture during the time of Messiah.

We know that Jesus was still in Perea, because in verse 1 of this chapter, He was in the "land beyond Jordan." We can also see that the Pharisees were the ones who started the issue here, as they came to Jesus tempting Him, saying, "Is it lawful for a man to put away his wife for *every* cause?" We can see here the main problem that caused Jesus to answer the way He did. The Pharisees had created their own ideas of what the Old Testament Scriptures said about divorce.

We must read the law concerning divorce in Deuteronomy 24:1–2: "When a man hath taken a wife, and married her, and it come to pass that she find no favour in his eyes, because he hath found some uncleanness in her: then let him write her a bill of divorcement, and give it in her hand, and send her out of his house. And when she is departed out of his house, she may go and be another man's wife." So there was a biblical law of divorce under certain situations. What were they? If the man found out that his wife had been with another man, or if the woman committed spiritual idolatry, as was the case in Ezra 10, a divorce could be granted.

But divorce was never meant to be a license to abuse women. The Pharisees were taking advantage of their wives by divorcing them for "every cause." In the time of Jesus, if a woman left the house to get a job, she could be divorced. If she refused to have intercourse with her husband, she could be divorced. If the husband found a prettier woman, he would sometimes just divorce his wife in order to get a better looking wife. If the woman was not a good cook, she could be divorced. There were over a dozen reasons the Pharisees used for divorcing their wives. But listen to what the Messiah said to them: "Have you never read, that he which made them at the beginning made them male and female. And said, for this cause shall a man leave father and mother, and shall cleave to his wife; and they twain shall be one flesh? Wherefore they are no more twain, but one flesh. What therefore God hath joined together, let no man put asunder."

Jesus took them back to what God intended from the beginning, before sin came into the world. God intended for a marriage to be for life. And just because a provision was made for divorce, did not give them the right to have a hard heart toward their wives. Jesus told them they were committing adultery, unless sexual *fornication* had been proven (vs. 9). Jesus was *not* saying that divorce was a sin — he would have been going against His own law. He was condemning the Pharisees for abusing the law of divorcement. (Read Jeremiah 3 where God even divorced Israel for their spiritual adultery.)

Then the disciples made a good statement. "If the case of the man be so with his wife [if fornication has been committed], it is not good to marry." Jesus gave a strange answer, one that we seldom ever hear in our Church world. He brought up the absence of the physical need to be married. Some men were *born* eunuchs (men who have no genitals). Some men were *made* eunuchs by other men. Some men *made themselves* eunuchs for the kingdom of heaven. In other words, some men have no physical need for a wife any longer. That's not the only reason for a wife, but it is *a* reason, that Jesus gave. As we look at the writings of Paul in 1 Corinthians 7, we can see this emphasis as well. Maybe one of the reasons there are so many divorces today is because the Church has not done a good job explaining the responsibilities to men and women before they get married.

Divorce scars people, hurts precious little children, and I would have to be against it in most cases. However, this self-righteous attitude that says divorce is always a sin, and that divorced people cannot serve in the Church is biblically wrong. Divorce sometimes happens to innocent people, who didn't desire it in the first place. When the qualifications are given for bishops and deacons, it says they must be "a husband of one wife," which means "a one-woman man." It has nothing to do with divorce or remarriage. Many people have been mistreated in the Church over the years because of biblical ignorance.

FORGIVENESS AND SERVICE

Luke 17:1–6   The Messiah gave the disciples some very important lessons about forgiveness and service, in these few verses. He begins by saying that it is impossible to live in this world without people offending us in some way. "It were better for him that a millstone were hanged about his neck, and he cast into the sea, than that he should offend one of these little ones." These words were spoken by Jesus back in Capernaum, when He had a little child in His arms. It is a sinful world, filled with many lost individuals. But our Lord is talking here about a brother who offends us, and what we must do.

If a believing brother offends us and we go to him, if he repents, we are to forgive him. If he offends us seven times in one day, and if he repents, we are to forgive him. It's that simple. When the disciples heard this, they knew their faith was weak, and they said to the Lord, "Increase our faith." Jesus closed the lesson by saying, "If ye had faith as a grain of mustard seed, ye might say unto this sycamine tree, Be thou plucked up by the root, and be thou planted in the sea; and it should obey you." In other words, real faith in Messiah will give us the power to forgive our offending brothers and sisters. We all have mountains in our lives that need to be removed, so to speak. When there is a mountain of unforgiveness in our way, through faith, we can remove it. Praise God!

Matt. 18:21–35

Sometimes we are like the servant who owed a certain king 10,000 talents. After he fell down and asked the king for mercy, and to have patience with him, the king had compassion on him and forgave him the debt. But then, that same servant went out and found one of his fellow servants, who owed him just 100 pence. The servant who had been forgiven for his great debt, took his fellow servant by the throat and said, "Pay me what thou owest." The fellow servant fell down at his feet, and asked him to have mercy on him, but the servant cast him into prison. When the king found out about it, he was angry, and told him that after he had been forgiven that great debt, he should have shown forgiveness to his fellow servant. The king turned him over to the tormentors, until he could pay his own debt.

The lesson for us is very clear, after all that Jesus the Messiah has forgiven us, we should show forth forgiveness to others. The reason people do not forgive others is that they have never received Christ's forgiveness for themselves. Once we have seen the Father's love and mercy, we will extend it to those around us.

Luke 17:7–10

Then Jesus gave a parable about serving in His kingdom. The parable was given about having a servant plowing or feeding cattle, and when he had come from the field, would the master let him sit down to eat before he ate? No, the master would have the servant serve him first, and then he could eat and drink. Would the master thank the servant for what he had done? No, that was his hired job to do. "So likewise ye, when ye shall have done all those things which are commanded you, say, We are unprofitable servants: we have done that which was our duty to do." The word used here for "unprofitable" is *achreios* — "useless" or "undeserving."

We should feel so honored to serve in God's kingdom that we would not want thanks or recognition. If it were not for His grace and mercy, we would be forever lost. For Him to save us, then put us in His service, we should feel humbled to think that the God of the universe wants to use us. So many want to be seen for their works, like the Pharisees of Jesus' day. I feel as though I am the least of God's servants, and I feel so unworthy to do what I do for Him. When I think back on my life, and realize how far He has brought me, it is my reasonable service to give Christ my very best. God is not looking for entertainers, but true servants. The word in Hebrew is *ebed*, which means "bondman." May we be found serving the Messiah — that is our duty.

GIVING GOD
THE GLORY

Luke 17:11–19   As Jesus the Messiah was journeying to Jerusalem, He passed through Samaria one last time. As He entered into a certain village, ten lepers were standing afar off. They cried out, "Jesus, Master, have mercy on us." Jesus told them to go show themselves unto the priests. As they went on their way, they were cleansed. Jesus was probably giving the priests a sign that He truly was the Messiah. No Jewish leper had ever been cleansed in the history of Israel before the Messiah came. This was a Messianic miracle, and the priests should have known.

But the main lesson of the story is that only one of the ten lepers came back to thank the Lord for healing him, and he was a Samaritan. We can almost hear the sadness in Jesus' voice, as He asked, "Were there not ten cleansed? But where are the nine?" It was only the Samaritan, who was privileged to hear these words, "Arise, go thy way; thy faith hath made thee whole." Were the other nine truly saved, or were they just healed physically? There is one thing we do know — only the one who returned to give Him thanks was pleasing to Christ.

What a great lesson for all who have been touched by our Lord. Have we turned back to give Him thanks? How long has it been since we stopped and gave glory to God for the mighty works that He has done? The Lord wants us to love Him and to thank Him, for His love for us. It's not that the Lord is so weak that *He needs* our thanks, but He knows that *we need* it. When we give Him glory, there is something that builds up within us. We learn what life is all about, that it's an opportunity to have fellowship with God, through our faith in the Messiah. Once we learn to give Him the glory, then we are not so much concerned about drawing attention to ourselves. We were created for His glory, and He wants to hear it from us.

It's interesting to me that this one leper who turned back to thank Jesus was a Samaritan. We have in the Gospel accounts the story of the Samaritan woman; the story of the Good Samaritan; the time the disciples wanted to destroy some Samaritans, but Jesus rebuked them; and here, the grateful Samaritan. We must see here that God is showing the Jewish disciples that the people they despise the most, the Samaritans, will sometimes be the ones who will serve Him the greatest. The kingdom of God is not just for the Jew, it also is for the Gentile.

The Christ:

WHERE IS THE KINGDOM?

Luke 17:20–21
Luke 19:11

We have been looking at the characteristics of a person who is in God's kingdom. Now, we will look at where that Kingdom is. According to Luke 19:11, the Jews thought the Kingdom was going to appear, and the nation of Israel would be delivered from the Romans. They saw only one coming of the Messiah, and did not understand the suffering Messiah first, then the reigning Messiah. So they were looking for a Kingdom to be set up with all the splendor that many of the old Hebrew prophets had foretold. With this background, the Pharisees wanted to know when the Kingdom was coming.

Listen to what Jesus said: "The kingdom of God cometh not with observation; neither shall they say, Lo here! or, lo there! For, behold, the kingdom of God is *within you*." The Lord was telling them that the kingdom of God is in your midst even now. The Kingdom had been rejected by the nation as a whole, for they had rejected their king Messiah. So now, the Kingdom would not come with outward show — that was postponed until the Second Coming. The Kingdom would be in the hearts of the people. The Pharisees certainly didn't have the Messiah living inside of them, but the ones who believed Yeshua was the Messiah had the spiritual Kingdom already. The apostle Paul mentions this miracle in 2 Corinthians 6:16, that God would dwell inside His people. There are numerous verses in the old Hebrew Scriptures that testify to this promise. So what can we learn from this?

God does not live in buildings (Acts 7:48–50, 17:24); He lives in human beings. The kingdom of God is not in denominations, religious institutions, or elaborate church buildings. God lives inside of

His children. Through our child-like faith in Yeshua as the Messiah, the Holy Spirit comes to indwell our lives. If we are one of God's children, the kingdom of God is inside. What is so sad, just like the Pharisees of old, is that many are looking for an outward Kingdom, and they fail to see their need to be transformed by God's saving power.

The kingdom of God will come one day with outward show (Isa.11, Matt. 19:28, Acts 1:6), but only the ones who have the spiritual Kingdom within will enjoy the physical Kingdom on earth.

BARTIMAEUS AND ZACCHAEUS

Mark 10:46–52   We now leave the Perean ministry of the Messiah, and stop off at the oldest city in the world, Jericho, or *Yericho*. Here we can see the awesome compassion of our Lord as He passes through the city. No one could stop Him from going up to Jerusalem to die on the Cross, not even Satan himself. But here, our wonderful Lord *"stands still,"* for one blind man on the side of the road. When Jesus called for Bartimaeus, *Bar-timai*, he cast aside his garment and came to Jesus. Jesus asked him a question that has always touched me deeply, "What wilt thou that I should do unto thee?" The blind man said, "Lord, that I might receive my sight." And Jesus said unto him, "Go thy way; thy faith hath made thee whole." And immediately he received his sight, and followed Jesus in the way.

Jesus knew what was wrong with the man, but He wanted to hear his plea. At other times, the Messiah would touch their eyes, but here He just spoke the word. Jesus didn't want the disciples or anyone else to worship a particular method, but to worship Him!

Healing the blind was a Messianic miracle — no one could open the eyes of the blind but Messiah (Isa. 35:5; John 9:32). This poor blind man of Jericho heard that Jesus of Nazareth was passing by, and he knew that he was the long-awaited Messiah of Israel. A blind man could see more than the religious people could see. This was the lesson from John 9:39–41.

When the blind man received his sight, he immediately started following the Lord. Once a person has met the Master, they are never the same. Christianity is not trying to do your best to get to heaven, it is being touched by the King of heaven, and once we see Him for who He is, we follow Him all the days of our life. Many people who see physically have never seen spiritually. Just like Jesus opened Bartimaeus's eyes that day, we must tell Him what we need. If we need to be saved, we must acknowledge our need of Him. He is asking us that same question today: "What is it that I can do for you?"

Luke 19:1–10

When we take our tours to Israel each year, we pass through Jericho, and there we see a large, old, sycamore tree that stands today as a memorial to the story of *Zakkai*, Zacchaeus. We know that he was a publican who was hated by the Jews for collecting taxes for the Romans. He had gotten his wealth from robbing the common people. As Jesus was passing through the city, Zacchaeus wanted to see this man he had heard so much about. He was a short man, so he had to climb up a sycamore tree to look over the multitude of people. When Jesus passed by, He saw Zacchaeus up the tree and said to him, "Zacchaeus, make haste, and come down: for to day I must abide at thy house." All the people murmured because Jesus went to the house of a publican. After he met Jesus, he said, " Behold, Lord, the half of my goods I give to the poor; and if I have taken any thing from any man by false accusation, I restore him fourfold." And Jesus said unto him, "This day is salvation come to this house, forasmuch as he also is a son of Abraham. For the Son of man is come to seek and to save that which was lost."

When we look at Exodus 22:1, we find that under the old Jewish law, if someone stole a sheep, they were to pay them back with four sheep. This is why Zacchaeus said what he did. He was a Jew, of the seed of Abraham, but now he was a *spiritual* child of Abraham. When salvation comes to one's house, they will see their wrongs and try to make them right. Jesus forgives us of all of our mistakes, but salvation brings about a change. Even though we cannot live good enough to be saved, our works prove that we have been saved. Like Matthew, the publican Zacchaeus never took money from the common people again wrongfully. I believe that when we get to heaven we will see so many people that once were thieves, adulterers, and murderers, but were changed by the mighty Messiah!

The Laborers in the Vineyard

Matthew 20:1–16   This parable holds a gold mine of instruction to all who are trying to serve the Messiah. The important thing to remember is that the very first verse says, "For the kingdom of heaven is like. . . ." This is a picture of people who are working for God! To keep us from becoming self-righteous or prideful about our abilities, or how long we have served, Jesus speaks, and let's lend an ear.

A man who was a householder, went out early one morning to hire some laborers in his vineyard. The agreement would be for one penny, *denarius,* per day. He hired some that started at the third hour, 9:00 a.m., some started at the sixth hour, noon, some started at 3:00 p.m., and some started at the last hour of the day, the eleventh hour, 5:00 p.m. All agreed to work for one denarius.

When the evening came, the lord of the vineyard told his servant to pay every laborer his wages. Each one, beginning from the early morning workers to the late evening workers, received the same pay, one denarius.

The ones who had worked all day began to murmur and complain, because the ones who only worked one hour received the same as they did from working all day. The lord of the vineyard said, "Friend, I do thee no wrong: didst thou not agree with me for a penny? Take that thine is, and go thy way: I will give unto this last, even as unto thee. Is it not lawful for me to do what I will with mine own? Is thine *eye evil*, because I am good?" Jesus then added, "So the last shall be first, and the first last: for many be called but few chosen." The term "evil eye" was given to people in the time of Jesus who were miserly and greedy (Matt. 6:23).

The Lord's economy does not work like the world's. It's not how long someone has served in His kingdom that counts, it's what we do with the time we have. Some people have served for many years, but maybe their love and devotion to the Lord was not as much as someone who has served for just one year. So many people become prideful about how many years they have been saved, or how many years they have worked in the Church. God controls our heartbeats, He can end our lives whenever He chooses. If it were not for His mercy we could not exist. There are those who have served Christ for a short time, but they have been very effective. It's not *how long* we have served, or *how old* we are, that makes us worthy, it is the precious blood of Jesus that makes us righteous. Many who think they will be first in the kingdom will be last when it comes to rewards. Many who think they are last will be first.

We should never be intimidated by others because they have been a Christian for many years. God has a work for us to do, and if we are faithful, no matter how long that time span is, we will be rewarded. It's never too late to get enlisted in God's army!

THE WOMAN
TAKEN IN ADULTERY

John 8:1–11   We now leave the Perean ministry of the Messiah and follow Jesus to Jerusalem, in the account from the Gospel of John. Each narrative has its own uniqueness, and the Gospel of John was written later, close to the end of the first century. Through the inspiration of the Holy Spirit (John 14:26), John wrote down some things that were not recorded in the other three Gospels. Here is one of those happenings in the life of the Messiah that has been overlooked by many.

We can see that Jesus was on the Mount of Olives, He walked down that beautiful mountain, east of Jerusalem, and came into the temple, early in the morning. People came to Him, and He sat down and began teaching. It was customary for a rabbi to be seated while teaching others.

Here come the scribes and Pharisees again, bringing a woman who was caught in the very act of adultery. They wanted Jesus to accuse the sinful woman, and order them to stone her, as was written in the law of Moses. But Yeshua did something very strange, He wrote with His finger on the ground, and made as though He was ignoring them. So let's look at what the law of Moses said in Leviticus 20:10: "And the man that committeth adultery with another man's wife, even he that committeth adultery with his neighbor's wife, the *adulterer* and the *adulteress* shall be put to death." This could have been what Jesus wrote on the ground. This condemned the man and the woman. Then they continued asking Him, and Jesus said, "He that is without sin among you, let him first cast a stone at her." Jesus stooped down and wrote on the ground the second time. This time the scribes and Pharisees were convicted by their own conscience, and one by one they departed. The ones Jesus condemned were the religious leaders, not the adulteress woman. Listen to these words found in Jeremiah 17:13: "O Lord, the hope of Israel, all that forsake thee shall be ashamed, and they that depart from me *shall be written in the earth*, because they have forsaken the Lord, the fountain of living waters." The Pharisees had rejected Yeshua as the Messiah; this sinful woman realized her need for forgiveness.

Jesus did not condone her sin, He forgave her, and told her, "Go and sin no more." Her sin was evident, but Jesus had given her a new beginning. This is what happens when our sins are brought to God. Instead of us receiving condemnation, we receive God's mercy through the Messiah. Once we have been accepted by God, the power of the Holy Spirit comes into our lives, and we are changed. "Old things are passed away, all things are become new."

I Am the Light of the World

John 8 and 9   One of the three feasts that all Jews were required to attend was the Feast of Tabernacles. During this feast, four huge lampposts were erected in the Court of the Women, at the temple. Each was 75 feet high, with four bowls at the top, each bowl containing ten gallons of oil. The wicks were made from the soiled garments of the priests. These 16 enormous lamps would light up the entire courtyard in Jerusalem. Every religious Jew knew the significance of these lamps. They represented the presence of God among the Israelites in the wilderness. The Shekinah glory of God had followed the children of Israel in the cloud.

So here, Yeshua compares himself to these magnificent lamps and declares, " I am the light of the world," *"Anee or hah o lam."* Jesus is claiming to be the Shekinah glory! In other words, Jesus was claiming to be God! Jesus is the light that illuminates a person's way and, without Him, we all will walk in darkness.

Without the light of Christ, people have no sense of direction, why they are here, or where they are going. The religious Pharisees were spiritually blind and could not see that Jesus was their Messiah. We must have physical light to exist on earth, and we must have spiritual light to exist spiritually. These Pharisees could see physically, but they were blind to the things of God. They thought they were Abraham's children, simply because they were born a Jew. Jesus told them something that predated himself, "Verily, Verily, I say unto you, before Abraham was, I am." Jesus was saying that Abraham saw the day of the Messiah coming, and he rejoiced to see it. If they had been true children of Abraham, they would have known who the Messiah was.

It's interesting that they were not able to cast a stone at the adulteress woman, because they were guilty themselves, but here they were so blind that they took up stones to throw at Jesus. Can you imagine someone so blind that they would throw rocks at the Son of God?

Then, to further press home the message, Jesus heals a man that was born blind, illustrating how blind the Pharisees were and that He was the only Messiah! No one had ever healed someone *born* blind (John 9:32), so this miracle was a "Messianic miracle." We are all *born* into sin, and Jesus the Christ shines His light into our dark hearts so we can see what life is about.

When the Light came to Jerusalem, they were living in darkness, and rejected that Light. That's why Jesus started His ministry in Galilee, where the people felt their need of Him, and were not satisfied in their traditions. The words of Jesus are so needed in our world today: "I am the light of the world: he that followeth me shall not walk in darkness, but shall have the light of life."

I Am the Good Shepherd

John 10:1–18 is one of the most-loved passages, and contains two of the "I am" sayings of the Messiah. "I am the good shepherd," *"Anee hah ro eh hah tov,"* and "I am the door," *"Anee hah shah ar."* This would have been the way Jesus would have said them.

What is the background to the text? The blind man in John 9, whom Jesus healed, has been cast out by the religious leaders, and Jesus has found him and brought him to real faith in *who* He is. With this man being cast out, Jesus gives the *contrast* between the Jewish leaders and himself.

The Pharisees and scribes were thieves and robbers, and would not come through the door into the sheepfold. They thought their man-made traditions and their strict outward rituals would place them in God's kingdom.

The analogy of the shepherd and the sheep is the most often used in the Holy Bible. Jesus is saying here that He is the true Shepherd, the religious leaders were the false shepherds, and their deeds proved they were false.

Jesus says He is the door, and if any man will enter through Him, they shall be saved. The imagery here is so wonderful. In the time of Jesus, sheepfolds were simple walls of stone to keep the sheep at night. The opening of the sheepfold is where the shepherd would sit. He would become the actual door himself. Nothing could harm the sheep, as long as the shepherd stood guard. No sheep could enter or leave, without going through the shepherd. When someone goes through Jesus, the door, they become one of His sheep, and they shall go in and out and find pasture.

"The thief cometh . . . to kill, and to destroy" (John 10:10). Satan and his shepherds will not take care of the sheep, they are hirelings, only interested in the money they are making. One of the great verses in John's gospel is, "I am come that they might have life, and that they might have it more abundantly." Not only eternal life when our earthly life is over, but the abundant life while living on earth. How is that possible? By the Good Shepherd giving His life for the sheep. A person who is hired to watch the sheep will let the wolf get them. The Messiah came to really *give* His life for the sheep, not to *act* out the part.

The sheep hear the voice of the Good Shepherd, like this blind man had heard Jesus, and worshiped Him. Jesus says in John 10:16, He has other sheep which are not of this fold, talking about the Gentiles. But there is only one fold, and only one Shepherd. No one will take the Shepherd's life, He will lay it down, and then He will live again.

We know that it was in the winter time, according to verse 22, and the Feast of Dedication was being celebrated. This was the Feast of Hanukkah, a man-made feast, not a God-given feast. This lasted for eight days, and it helped the Jewish people remember when, in 167 B.C., the Syrian king Antiochus Epiphanes defiled the temple in Jerusalem, and Judas Maccabeus led a revolt, and overthrew the Syrian army. This was a tremendous victory for the Jewish people. This feast was celebrated in November and December each year. This is when the Messiah was in Jerusalem, and spoke these words.

One of the most assuring things Jesus ever said is recorded here, in John 10:27–30, "My sheep hear my voice, and I know them, and they follow me: And I give unto them eternal life; and they shall never perish, neither shall any man pluck them out of my hand. My Father, which gave them me, is greater than all; and no man is able to pluck them out of my Father's hand. I and my Father are one."

I will have to admit, that the doctrine of *eternal security* has been misrepresented in many circles within the Church. Saying that once a person is saved and no matter what they do they are still saved sometimes gives people the idea that it is okay to live however they choose to live, with a false sense of security. But the doctrine of eternal security is one that Jesus taught and, as a matter of fact, He taught double eternal security. The sheep are safe in *His* hands, and they are safe in the *Father's* hands. Where people get off track is when they try to mix works and grace together. No one can, or ever will, be able to live good enough to be saved. Salvation is of the Lord, and it all depends on *His* death on the cross, and *His* resurrection. The sheep may go astray from time to time, but if they are truly His sheep, they will always be His sheep. This idea that a person can be born again, then unborn, is ridiculous. When we meet the Savior, we are never the same anymore. How can anyone live a victorious life for Christ, if they do not *know* they are saved? Jesus will save a person, and they will *know* it!

When we study the life of a shepherd in Bible times, the 23rd Psalm has to be one of the most beautiful passages. "The Lord is

my Shepherd; I shall not want. He maketh me to lie down in *green pastures;* He leadeth me beside the *still waters*. He restoreth my soul; He leadeth me in the paths of righteousness *for His name's sake*. Yea, though I walk through the *valley of the shadow of death*, I will fear no evil; for thou art with me; thy rod and thy staff they comfort me. Thou *preparest a table* before me in the presence of mine enemies; thou *anointest my head with oil*; my cup runneth over. Surely goodness and mercy *shall follow me* all the days of my life; and I will dwell in the house of the Lord forever."

David emphasizes that it is the Lord who is his Shepherd. He takes care of all of his needs. He goes out and finds the northern, dewy, slopes, where the green grass is, and makes the sheep to lie down and rest in the middle of the day. Sheep cannot drink in swift water or they will drown, so the Lord finds them still water. The righteous paths that He leads them in, is for *His* name's sake, not for their name's sake. Death will come, but it is only a shadow, and the fear has been taken away. The rod protects the sheep, and the staff reaches and pulls them out of trouble. The sheep can even eat with their enemies, because the Lord has taught them how to forgive others. The sheep's faces are anointed with olive oil, to keep the flies from going up their nose, and eating their brains out. The Lord anoints His sheep with the Holy Spirit, to keep Satan out of their lives. The sheep are so filled with joy, that their cup is running over with thankfulness. The goodness and mercy of the Lord will follow, *radaph* (run after, hunt down), me all the days of my life. I am secure with my future, because He has promised me, that I shall dwell in His house forever.

It's time for God's sheep to *praise the Lord!*

MARTHA AND MARY

Luke 10:38–42   We now come to a village on the eastern slope of the Mount of Olives called Bethany, *Beit-an-yah*, "house of poverty." The Messiah came to the house where two sisters lived, Martha, *Marta*, and Mary, *Miryam*.

First of all, before we start trying to criticize Martha, we need to see her goodness. Her name in Hebrew means "lady," and she certainly loved our Lord, and received Him gladly. But there is a great lesson for us to learn from Martha and Mary.

Martha, being a lady, started serving Jesus, while Mary was sitting at His feet, listening to His words. Martha became upset because Mary was not helping her, so she told the Lord, "Lord, dost thou not care that my sister hath left me to serve alone? Bid her therefore that she help me." There wasn't anything wrong with what Martha was doing, she was serving Jesus! What a wonderful place Israel would have been, if all the people had greeted Jesus the way Martha did. What a wonderful world we would be living in, if everyone welcomed Yeshua into their homes like Martha did. But here is the lesson that Jesus gave to Martha, and we will do well to listen.

Jesus said, "Martha, Martha, thou art careful and troubled about many things; but one thing is needful: and Mary hath chosen that good part, which shall not be taken away from here." The Messiah was moving quickly toward His death in Jerusalem; it would be only a few days for Him to speak to His servants while on earth. What Jesus had to say was urgent, what Jesus had to say was life-changing, and He wanted His people to hear all they could while He was in their presence.

Martha was so preoccupied that she had forgotten the *most* important thing — *listening* to Jesus. Physical food was important, but spiritual food was *more* important. Remember what Jesus told the disciples when they returned from Samaria, and they said, "Master, eat." Then Jesus said, "I have meat to eat that ye know not of." Like most of us, Martha was more concerned about the physical food. But Mary was "eating His flesh, and drinking His blood," and was allowing Jesus to live inside of her spirit.

How many times are we so busy doing so-called good things that we miss spending time with the precious Savior? Life is too short for us to waste all of our energy on the physical things that will soon fade away. If we do not feed our spiritual lives with God's Word, then we will end up living a very carnal, Christian life (John 6:56). We need to be more like Mary, and sit at the feet of Jesus, every time we can. Mary realized her time with Jesus was passing quickly, and she wanted to learn what she could.

So let's leave this moving scene with two great thoughts:

1) It's *good* to be working *for* Jesus.
2) But it's *better* to be *with* Jesus.

THE RAISING
OF LAZARUS

John 11:1–44   Whenever Jesus would visit the little
village of Bethany, he felt at home when he stayed with His friends
there: Mary, Martha, and Lazarus.

Lazarus was sick, and the two sisters sent someone to tell Jesus.
Jesus told them, "This sickness is not unto death, but for the glory of
God, that the Son of God might be glorified thereby." What a touching chapter this is, and what makes it so precious is that it is recorded,
"Jesus loved Martha, and her sister, and Lazarus." Jesus was down by
the Jordan River where John first baptized (John 10:40–42), and He
waited two days after He was told about Lazarus. The disciples didn't
want Jesus to go back so close to Jerusalem, because the Jews had already said they wanted to stone Him. Jesus told them that a man who
walks in the light will not stumble, it's the ones who walk in darkness
that will fall.

Jesus told His disciples, "Our friend Lazarus sleepeth: but I go,
that I may awake him out of sleep." When the disciples heard that,
they thought he was talking about Lazarus taking a restful nap, but
Jesus said, "Lazarus is dead." Jesus deliberately waited two days, so
that Lazarus would be dead, so the disciples and others would believe
on Him.

In the middle of all of this, one of the disciples named Thomas,
T'oma, "twin," spoke up and said, "Let us go, that we may die with
Him." The term "doubting Thomas" doesn't fit this time.

When Jesus came to Bethany, He found that Lazarus had been
dead four days. It was Jewish custom that after a person had been

dead four days, the body was pronounced legally dead, and the body had started to corrupt.

Many of the Jews were coming to the house of Mary and Martha to comfort them, and when Martha heard that Jesus was coming, she left the house and went out to meet Jesus. Mary stayed at the house mourning, *shi-vah* (seven days of mourning after a family member died). Martha told Jesus that if He had been there, Lazarus would not have died. Jesus said, "Thy brother shall rise again." Martha thought Jesus was talking about the resurrection day, but here are the words that Jesus told Martha, "I am the resurrection and the life: he that believeth in me, though he were dead, yet shall he live. And whosoever liveth and believeth in me shall never die. Believest thou this?" Jesus is saying that our faith in Him gives us a new life, and that life will never perish. Here Martha makes one of the great statements recorded in the gospels, "Yea, Lord: I believe that thou art the Christ, the Son of God, which should come into the world."

Martha ran back home and told Mary that the Master was calling for her. Although the Jews that were comforting Mary in the house thought that Mary was going to the grave of Lazarus to weep, she went straight to Jesus, which was a little distance from Bethany. When Mary saw Jesus, she fell down at His feet. Mary was always kneeling at the feet of Jesus, what a place to be! (Luke 10:39; John 12:3).

She also told the Lord that if He had been there, Lazarus would not have died. When Jesus saw Mary weeping and the Jews that had followed her weeping, "He groaned in the spirit, and was troubled." Try to imagine Jesus, groaning in the spirit. When they told Jesus to come and see where they had laid Lazarus, "Jesus wept"! The shortest verse in the Bible, yet the most moving. God became a man, not *just* to die, but to know every emotion that we humans feel. What a picture, tears flowing from the eyes of Jesus the Messiah!

The Jews that were there comforting the two sisters saw how much Jesus loved Lazarus. They knew He had opened the eyes of the blind, and they wondered why Jesus would have let Lazarus die. Opening the eyes of the blind was considered a greater miracle than raising the dead.

As Jesus was coming to the grave of Lazarus, He groaned again in His spirit. It was a cave, and a stone was placed upon it. He told them to take away the stone. Martha spoke up and said, "Lord, by this time he stinketh: for he hath been dead four days." Jesus told her, "Said I not unto thee, that, if thou wouldest believe, thou shouldest see the glory of God?" Then they took the stone away, and Jesus lifted His eyes, and said, "Father, I thank thee that thou hast heard me, and I knew that thou hearest me always: but because of the people which stand by I said it, that they may believe that thou hast sent me." Then He cried, "Lazarus, come forth." Lazarus came out of the grave, and Jesus said, "Loose him, and let him go."

Almost an entire chapter is given to this miracle of Lazarus being raised from the dead. I'm reminded of the passage in Luke 16:31 where Abraham told the rich man in hell, "If one rose from the dead," some people would still not believe. It's interesting that the poor beggar who died and went to Abraham's bosom was also a man named Lazarus. This miracle would cause a tremendous stir among the religious leaders. In verse 53, from that day forth, they joined together to put Jesus to death. And because many of the Jews were believing in Jesus, because of the miracle of Lazarus, they wanted to kill Lazarus also (John 12:9–11).

We can see at least three things here:

1) God's purpose — *for His glory*, verse 4
2) God's love — *Jesus wept*, verse 35
3) God's power — *"Lazarus come forth,"* verse 43

This miracle was a prefigure of the Lord's *own* resurrection, except Lazarus would eventually have to die again physically, but our Messiah would only have to die once! What Jesus told Martha, will stand the test of time, "I am the resurrection and the life," *"Anee ha te chee ya veh hah cha yeem."*

THE SUPPER
AT BETHANY

John 12:1–8
Matthew 26:6–13
Mark 14:3–9
I suppose if Jesus had raised one of our brothers from the dead, we would have given Him a supper as well. Furthermore, if we had been the one whom He raised, we would *certainly* be at that supper.

We find in John's Gospel, Martha serving Jesus *again*, and Lazarus, whom Jesus had just raised from the dead, sitting at the table. Can we start to imagine all the things that were going through their minds? What were they talking about? What were the expressions on their faces? What a moment in time — Jesus sitting at the table, in a little poor village, with His friends.

Here we see Mary — you remember Mary don't you, the one who was sitting at His feet back in Luke 10:39? Mary understood the teachings of Jesus more than the disciples did, concerning His death and resurrection. She had listened!

Because of her true love for the Messiah, she suddenly takes a pint of expensive ointment (about a year's wages, 300 denarius), and anoints the head and feet of Jesus (Matt. 26:7). She took her hair, and wiped the precious feet of our Lord. The house was filled with the sweet odor of the ointment.

The disciples, especially Judas Iscariot, thought that what Mary did was a waste of money. I love what Jesus told the disciples, "Let her alone. . . . She hath done what she could: she is come aforehand to anoint my body to the burying" (Mark 14:6–8). Mary knew more about the Messiah's mission than any of the disciples at this point. She was anointing His body in preparation for His burial.

The Christ:

There will always be someone trying to discourage us when we are worshiping our Lord. Even when others think that we have gone to the *extreme*, The Lord still deserves our very best. What a wonderful thought, to think that one day Jesus might say to me, *"He did what He could."*

THE TRIUMPHAL ENTRY OF MESSIAH

1) THE HEBREW PROPHECIES

Zechariah 9:9 Rejoice greatly, O daughter of Zion; shout, O daughter of Jerusalem: behold, thy King cometh unto thee: he is just, and having salvation; lowly, and riding upon an ass, and upon a colt the foal of an ass."

Psalm 8:2: "Out of the mouth of babes and sucklings hast thou ordained strength because of thine enemies, that thou mightest still the enemy and the avenger."

Ezekiel 11:23: "And the glory of the Lord went up from the midst of the city, and stood upon the mountain which is on the *east* side of the city."

Ezek. 43:2: "And behold, the glory of the God of Israel came from the way of the east."

2) THE HISTORICAL SITUATION

Matthew 21:1–17
Mark 11:1–10
Luke 19:29–38
John 12:12–19 This is such an important prophecy being fulfilled, that each Gospel narrative records it. The prophecy of Zechariah said that the Messiah would enter

Jerusalem riding a *donkey*. Ezekiel saw the glory of the Lord departing the temple, and returning to the temple from the *east*. Jesus entered Jerusalem from the *east*, coming in by way of Jericho and Bethany.

Three of the Gospel accounts tell us that the scene started at a place called Bethphage, *Beit-Pa-gei*, "house of unripe figs." It is interesting to note that this was the city limit for Jerusalem. The hour had to be just right — and was. He didn't come riding a white horse, but a lowly donkey, "whereon never man sat." Yeshua, being the God-man, had control over nature and over the animals. This donkey didn't try to throw Jesus, because the donkey knew the Creator was riding! In the time of Jesus, a king would ride a horse if he was bringing war, but he would ride a donkey if he was bringing peace. The Messiah was offering *true* peace to Jerusalem that day, but the nation rejected Him.

Jesus entered this world through a virgin girl, *who had never known a man.* He rode a donkey *that no one had ever ridden before.* He will be buried in a tomb, *where no man had ever been laid before.*

The people starting shouting praise to Jesus, *Hosanna,* "Please, deliver us!" laying palm branches in the way as a sign of being under His authority. Among the crowd were the people who were there when Jesus raised Lazarus on the other side of the Mount of Olives, Mary, Martha, Lazarus, and others. Much of the praise was coming as a result of that powerful miracle.

Some of the Pharisees told Jesus to rebuke His disciples. But Jesus said, "I tell you that, if these should hold their peace, the stones would immediately cry out."

When the Messiah came near the city of Jerusalem, He began to cry because Israel did not know the time of their visitation. What a sight it is to make the descent from the Mount of Olives, and behold the golden city of Jerusalem. This is always one of the highlights when we travel to the Holy Land.

Matthew's Gospel gives us the account of Jesus cleansing the temple the *second* time, which made the high priests even more angry, because they were getting rich off of the common people. Then we see the fulfillment of Psalm 8:2, when the children starting crying, "Hosanna to the son of David." The chief priests and scribes were very displeased. Then Jesus said, "Have you never read, out of the mouth of babes and sucklings thou hast perfected praise?"

3) THE SPIRITUAL APPLICATION

We were created to *praise God!* Even though the religious leaders did not believe in Jesus as the Messiah, and in spite of the powers of Rome, the common people shouted praise to Jesus. Even creation bows in worship to the Lord, and we should live our lives with praise on our lips. Until we learn how to worship the Messiah in our daily lives, we will never learn how to worship Him in our public churches. It's the humble, child-like people who God has ordained to bring Him the most praise. It dumbfounds the wise and prudent for the simple people to be giving praise to God, just like it did in the temple that day. God shuts up His enemies with "babes and sucklings."

The people who shouted "Hosannah" were *not* the same ones who shouted "Crucify Him," as many have thought. These people loved our Lord. It was the religious leaders that enlisted a mob for the crucifixion.

We can see again how important it is to *know* the Hebrew Scriptures. They *must* be fulfilled. We shall see the Scriptures really come together when we reach the death, burial, and resurrection of the Messiah.

PARABLE OF THE HOUSEHOLDER

Matthew 21:33–46   When the Messiah saw how the religious leaders were questioning His authority, He gave a parable that really brought forth the lack of spirituality of the nation of Israel, and their condemnation. This one was pointed directly toward them, and they understood.

The parable talks about a householder who planted a vineyard and put husbandmen in charge of it while he went into a far country.

The time for gathering the fruit drew near, and the householder sent his servants to the husbandmen to gather the fruits. The husbandmen beat one of the servants, killed another, and stoned another. The householder sent other servants, and they were killed as well. Last of all, the householder sent his son, hoping they would reverence his son. But the wicked husbandmen also killed the son.

What Yeshua was saying was, Israel had killed many of the great prophets, and rejected John the Baptist. Now they were going to kill the very Son of God!

Here, Jesus asked the religious leaders what the householder should do unto those husbandmen. Their answer predicts their own destruction. "He will miserably destroy those wicked men, and will let out his vineyard unto other husbandmen, which shall render him the fruits in their season."

These next three verses tell the lesson Jesus was trying to convey: "Jesus saith unto them, Did ye never read in the scriptures, The stone which the builders rejected, the same is become the head of the corner: this is the Lord's doing, and it is marvellous in our eyes? Therefore say I unto you, the kingdom of God shall be taken from you, and given to a nation bringing forth fruits thereof. And whosoever shall fall on this stone shall be broken: but on whomsoever it shall fall, it will grind him to powder." The Messiah had been rejected by Israel. They were not bringing forth any spiritual fruit. The kingdom would be given to the Gentiles, and this has been the tale of Christian history for almost two thousands years. The Messiah, "the stone that the builders rejected," would become the head cornerstone of the church, and "the stone," would one day crush the Gentile unbelievers. God will deal with Israel once again, when the "times of the Gentiles" has been fulfilled.

The religious leaders knew that Jesus was talking about them, and when He said that the Kingdom would be given to another nation, that was the straw that broke the camel's back.

RENDER UNTO GOD THE THINGS WHICH ARE GOD'S

Matthew 22:15–22
Mark 12:13–17
Luke 10:10–16

It's amazing that even groups of people who were normally enemies joined together against the Messiah. The Pharisees sent disciples together with the Herodians, trying to catch Jesus in something bad enough to give Him up to the Roman governor. When they said, "Neither carest thou for any man: for thou regardest not the person of men," this was a Hebrew idiom for not showing partiality. Jesus was no respecter of persons like the Pharisees were.

The question they asked Jesus was, "Is it lawful to give tribute unto Caesar, or not?" Jesus, knowing their wicked thoughts, said, "Shew me the tribute money." When they brought Him a denarius, He asked them, "Whose is this image and superscription?" They said, "Caesar's." Then here is one of the most remarkable sayings that Jesus ever gave, "Render therefore unto Caesar, the things which are Caesar's; and unto God the things that are God's."

What did Jesus mean? The denarius had an image of Caesar on the coin, and they were to give Caesar what was due. But the Pharisees and the Herodians were made in the image of God, and they were to give God back what was His! They were not giving God what was rightfully His.

Humans are made in God's image, and it is our reasonable service to give God our hearts and lives. Because Israel was under Roman rule, Caesar demanded his tribute money. But because all people are under God's rule, God demands proper service to Him. When we accept Jesus of Nazareth as the Messiah, His death on the Cross for our sins, that is the first *rendering*. His *payment* for our sins tells us that we are not our own, we have been bought with a price!

The Christ:

MESSIAH ANSWERS THE SADDUCEES

Matthew 22:23–33   One of the religious groups in Jesus' day was the Sadducees, or in Hebrew, *Tz'dukim*. They were the aristocrats of the day, and they did not believe in the resurrection (Acts 4:2). While all the other groups were tempting Jesus, they decided to get in on the action. But when someone comes to Jesus the Messiah, trying to trick Him with a question, *sh'eilah*, they will always lose the battle.

The Sadducees only believed in the first five books of the Bible, "the Torah." So here they come to Jesus with a very hypothetical question. Under the old Jewish law, if a man who was married died without having any children, his brother could marry the same woman in order to keep the bloodline to the next generation. The Sadducees asked Jesus, if this happened *seven* times, and the seven men and the woman died, whose wife would she be in the resurrection?

"Jesus answered and said unto them, Ye do err, not knowing the scriptures, nor the power of God. For in the resurrection they neither marry, nor are given in marriage, but are as the angels of God in heaven. But as touching the resurrection of the dead, have ye not read that which was spoken unto you by God, saying, I am the God of Abraham, and the God of Isaac, and the God of Jacob? God is not the God of the dead, but of the living."

The two grave errors with the Sadducees were that they did not know the Scriptures nor the power of God. These are the same problems that many people have today. In my travels over the years, I have found that the lack of Bible understanding has caused much of our problems in the churches. When someone does not know the power of God, how can they know how to live the Christian life?

Jesus told them that in the resurrection there will be no marriage. Marriage is a sacred institution, and should be honored by all, but it is an *earthly* institution. The reason there is a need for marriage on earth is that because people *die*, there needs to be procreation, but in the resurrection, people will *never die*.

Watch how Jesus turns the tables on the Sadducees. He takes a passage out of the Torah to prove that there *is* life after death. Abraham, Isaac, and Jacob, had been physically dead for hundreds of years. But Jesus was saying, God is still their God! God is not the God of the dead, but of the living!

What a thought, to know that when we get to heaven we will see Abraham, Isaac, Jacob, and all the Old Testament saints.

The Christ:

THE WIDOW'S MITE

Mark 12:41–44
Luke 21:1–4

In the days of Jesus, a "mite" or "lepton" was the smallest coin used. It took 128 of them to make one denarius, which was a day's wages. So a mite was 1/128 of a day's wage.

There was a trumpet-shaped box in the temple, and when someone cast in a lot of coins, it would make a loud sound. But when someone cast in just a little money, the sound would be soft. Jesus saw the rich men casting in their gifts, and He also saw a poor widow casting in two mites. And He said, "Of a truth I say unto you, that this poor widow hath cast in more than they all: For all these have of their abundance cast in unto the offerings of God; but she of her penury [*husterema*, "poverty"] hath cast in all the living that she had."

So we can easily see that Jesus was not impressed with all of the rich men giving their large gifts. It's not *how much* we give to promote the gospel, it's *how* we give. This poor widow gave out of her heart, and that's what counted.

We should not use this touching story to justify giving our least unto the Lord's work. This woman gave *all* she had. Have we given *all* we have? The Lord does not require us to give everything up, but we should live our lives in such a way that we know it all belongs to Him anyway. When we give, we should give from our hearts!

MATTHEW 24

Matthew 24:1–51   This chapter is one the great chapters in the Bible when it comes to studying about the end times. Much controversy has risen over the centuries about when certain things will happen. This work is not directed to that end. Our focus here is on the person of Messiah and His message. I will try to keep it brief and focus on the six sections that divide *part* of this tremendous sermon Jesus gave on the Mount of Olives.

Verses 1–2: As Jesus went out of the temple, and started walking up the slope on the Mount of Olives, He could look back and see the entire temple area. The disciples wanted Jesus to look at the grandeur of the temple. Jesus then predicted the destruction of Jerusalem. "There shall not be left here one stone upon another, that shall not be thrown down." This happened in A.D. 70 when Titus, the Roman emperor, besieged Jerusalem, and wanting all of the gold that was between the huge stones, they threw every stone down. All of the trees were cut down, and several hundred thousand Jews were killed, according to Flavius Josephus, the historian from the first century.

This was a major watershed for Christianity and Judaism. If this had not happened, then Christianity would have been a small sect *within* Judaism, and probably would have died in the first century. The old system had to be replaced. God no longer dwelt in buildings of stone, but in the hearts of His people, through faith in the Messiah Jesus.

Verse 3: As Jesus was sitting on the Mount of Olives, the disciples asked Him a threefold question: when shall these things be, what shall be the sign of thy coming, and the end of the world?

Verses 4–14: Regarding the end of the world, there are many signs to look for: false messiahs, wars and rumors of wars, famines, pestilences, and earthquakes, Messiah's followers will be hated, many will be offended, increase in false prophets, sin will increase, love will grow cold, only the ones who endure will be saved, and the gospel of the Kingdom must be preached unto all nations.

All of these things we can see in our world today. We have to be getting close to the end of the world!

Verses 15–26: Jesus mentions "the abomination of desolation" spoken of by the prophet Daniel. Why? Because what happened when Antiochus Epiphanes desecrated the temple in 167 B.C. was a picture of what will happen again, when the temple that will be built during the tribulation period is taken over by Satan, trying to overthrow God. The first time was by a Syrian king, the next time it will be by Satan. But God will intervene this time, at the end of the seven-year tribulation period. Many Bible scholars believe that the place where the Jews will flee during this terrible time will be the place mentioned in Isaiah 63:1, Bozrah (Petra). This will be a time more horrible than anything the world has ever seen. False prophets will rise with signs and wonders, deceiving many. This is the tribulation period!

Verses 27–31: The second coming of the Messiah will come out of the *east*. Wherever Israel will be, that's where the Gentiles will be gathered. Wonders in the sky will occur. The sun will be darkened. The moon will not give her light. The stars will fall, and the powers of the heavens shall be shaken. The Son of Man will come in clouds of glory (Acts 1:11; Rev. 19:11–16). The angels shall gather all of the elect from one end of heaven to the other.

Verses 32–51: One of the key verses is, "Verily I say unto you, this generation, *genea*, shall not pass, till all these things be fulfilled." The word "genea" means "race, stock, kind." The Jewish people will not vanish from the earth, until all things are fulfilled.

It will be like it was in the days of Noah and Lot (Matt. 24:37–39; Luke 17:28–29). People will be too preoccupied with pleasure, buying and selling, eating and drinking. They didn't listen to Noah, and they will turn a deaf ear to the gospel in the end. They were living in sexual perversion in the land of Sodom, and we can see a tremendous increase in homosexuality in our world today. This must truly be a sign that we are nearing the end. But I would like to call your attention to the last verse of Matthew 23, "For I say unto you, Ye shall not see me henceforth, till ye shall say, Blessed is he that cometh in the name of the Lord."

The number one sign to watch concerning the end time is the regathering of the Jews back to Israel. Over five million Jews are in the land today, more than at any other time in the history of the world. May I ask you, why did Israel become a nation just recently (1948)? Why are all these Jews coming back to the land *now*? Listen to a prophecy in Jeremiah 31:35–37: "Thus saith the Lord, which giveth the sun for a light by day, and the ordinances of the moon and of the stars for a light by night, which divideth the sea when the waves thereof roar; The LORD of hosts is his name: If those ordinances depart from before me, saith the LORD, then the seed of Israel also shall cease from being a nation before me for ever. Thus saith the LORD; if heaven above can be measured, and the foundations of the earth searched out beneath, I will also cast off all the seed of Israel for all that they have done, saith the LORD."

Israel will always be a nation, and when we see them gathering back into the land, we know they will soon say, "Blessed is he that cometh in the name of the Lord." The nation *rejected* the Messiah the first time, they will *believe* in Him the second time.

Jesus answered the disciples' three questions, and one of His answers we need to heed today: "Watch therefore: for ye know not what hour your Lord doth come."

The Ten Virgins —
A Test of Profession

Matthew 25:1–13   The Messiah had just given the disciples the answers to their questions concerning the end times. Now, He feels it is necessary to teach them the danger of *professing* to be saved, without *possessing* the Holy Spirit. Jesus gives two more parables about the kingdom of heaven.

This first parable deals with ten virgins who took their lamps and went forth to meet the bridegroom. Five of them were wise, and five were foolish. Why? The foolish virgins took no oil with them for their lamps, but the wise did take oil. While they were sleeping, the bridegroom came, and they heard the cry, "Behold, the bridegroom cometh; go ye out to meet him." While the foolish virgins were trimming their lamps, they realized they had no oil. They tried borrowing some oil from the wise virgins, but there was not enough for all of them. So while the foolish virgins were gone to buy some oil, the bridegroom came, and the wise virgins were ready, and they went in with him to the marriage. The foolish virgins came saying, "Lord, Lord, open to us. But he answered and said, Verily I say unto you, I know you not. Watch therefore, for ye know neither the day nor the hour wherein the Son of man cometh."

In the time of Jesus, they used small olive oil lamps, and the wicks were made out of flax. Olive oil was very accessible, but the foolish virgins thought because they had lamps, they would be ready. What is the lesson for us here?

1)   Having the lamp of profession is not enough. We may be moral (they were virgins), but just *professing* to know the Messiah

will not give us entrance into heaven. I'm reminded of what Jesus said back in Matthew 7:21, "Not every one that saith unto me, Lord, Lord, shall enter into the kingdom of heaven."

2) We must have the Holy Spirit. Olive oil here is a symbol of the blessed Holy Spirit. The one true evidence that we are saved is the indwelling Spirit. When a person is born again, God's spirit comes to live inside of them.

If we are not sure that we have the Holy Spirit, then we must go to God and tell Him we believe that Jesus is the Messiah, trust in His death and resurrection, and ask God to give us the Holy Spirit (Luke 11:13). We must not worry about what anyone thinks about us. If we join *many* churches and live a clean life and do not have the Holy Spirit, then we are lost. Just like olive oil was easily obtained, the Holy Spirit is easily obtained when we come as little children, believing and receiving the Messiah!

THE PARABLE OF THE TALENTS — A TEST OF SERVICE

Matthew 25:14–30   When the Messiah returns, there will be a revealing of who served the Kingdom, and who did not.

Here we see a man who was traveling into a far country, and delivered his goods to his servants. To one servant he gave *five* talents, to one servant he gave *two* talents, and to one servant he gave *one* talent. The servant who had five talents went and traded and gained five more talents. The man who had two talents went and gained two more talents. But the man who only had one talent went and buried his talent in the ground.

When the lord came back he had this to say to those servants who gained other talents: "Well done, thou good and faithful servant: thou hast been faithful over a few things, I will make thee ruler over many things: enter thou into the joy of thy lord."

To the servant who only had one talent, and buried it in the ground, he said: "Thou wicked and slothful servant. . . . Take therefore the talent from him, and give it unto him which hath ten talents."

Then Jesus closes the parable by saying, "For unto every one that hath shall be given, and he shall have abundance: but from him that hath not shall be taken away even that which he hath. And cast ye the unprofitable servant into outer darkness: there shall be weeping and gnashing of teeth."

What is the lesson? We must not feel belittled because we do not have many talents. It's what we do with what we have that will count. Sometimes people who have more talents were given them because the Lord knew they would use them for His kingdom. Some people, on the other hand, are so worried about saving and storing up for a rainy day, that they hide their talents to keep someone else from getting them. We are to *use* what we have, and the Lord is keeping a record! There will be a *test* when the Lord returns. May the Lord say unto us one day, "Well done, thou good and faithful servant."

MESSIAH'S RETURN — THE TEST OF THE NATIONS

Matthew 25:31–46 The Messiah Yeshua is using an analogy of sheep and goats to describe the judgment of the Gentile nations when He returns to earth. This judgment is different than the "Great White Throne" judgment that is mentioned in the Book of the Revelation. This scene is on earth. Jesus is talking about three classes of people: the sheep, the goats, and *"my brethren."* The brethren are the Jewish remnant who will preach the gospel of the Kingdom to all nations during the tribulation period.

This passage has been very misrepresented over the centuries, missing the proper context of the passage. As a shepherd divides his sheep from the goats, Jesus will set the sheep on His right hand, and the goats on the left. The sheep are the nations who showed compassion and love to the Jewish brethren during the tribulation. As they helped the brethren, they were actually helping the Lord himself. When the brethren were hungry, they fed them. When they were thirsty, they gave them drink. When they were strangers, they took them in. When they were naked, they clothed them. When they were sick and in prison, they visited them. Jesus said, "Verily I say unto you, Inasmuch as ye have done it unto one of the least of these my brethren, ye have done it unto me."

Those nations that will be placed on His left will be the ones who did not show compassion to the Jewish remnant during the tribulation. They did not feed them when they were hungry. They did not give them drink when they were thirsty. They did not take them in when they were strangers. They did not clothe them when they were naked. They did not visit them when they were sick and in prison. Jesus closes this section with a tremendous warning: "Verily I say unto you, Inasmuch as ye did it not to one of the least of these, ye did it not to me. And these shall go away into everlasting punishment; but the righteous into life eternal."

The lesson we can learn is that when we show compassion to the nation of Israel or the Jews, we will be blessed by God. The United States of America has been richly blessed over the years, because we have befriended Israel. When we stop supporting Israel, then America is finished.

THE BETRAYAL OF JUDAS

Prophecy

1) THE HEBREW PROPHECIES

Zechariah 11:12–13 "And I said unto them, If ye think good, give me my price; and if not, forebear. So they weighed for my price thirty pieces of silver. And the LORD said unto me, Cast it unto the potter: a goodly price that I was prised at of them. And I took the thirty pieces of silver, and cast them to the potter in the house of the LORD."

Psalm 41:9: "Yea, mine own familiar friend, in whom I trusted, which did eat of my bread, hath lifted up his heel against me."

Psalm 55:12–14: "For it was not an enemy that reproached me; then I could have borne it; neither was it he that hated me that did magnify himself against me; then I would have hid myself from him: But it was thou, a man mine equal, my guide, and mine acquaintance."

History

2) THE HISTORICAL SITUATION

Matthew 26:14–16
Mark 14:10–11
Luke 22:3–6 "Then one of the twelve, called Judas Iscariot, went unto the chief priests And said unto them, What will ye give me, and I will deliver him unto you? And they

covenanted with him for thirty pieces of silver. And from that time he sought opportunity to betray him."

This has to be one of the darkest moments in history, when one of the immediate 12 disciples, Judas Iscariot, sold out the Son of God. A man who walked with Jesus throughout His earthly ministry, and saw and heard all that Jesus did. He was also the one who kept the little bag of money for the disciples (John 12:6). So he was the treasurer for the little band, and this is where Satan got a stronghold.

After Judas realized what he had done, he went back to the temple, threw the 30 pieces of silver down, and went and hanged himself (Matt. 27:3–10). The actions of Judas fulfilled the prophecies of Zechariah 11:12–13, Psalm 41:9, and Psalm 55:12–14.

3) THE SPIRITUAL APPLICATION

Application

Just because someone is involved in ministry work does not mean they will not go shipwreck. We all must keep ourselves on the lookout for the devil to enter into our lives. If we do not stay in God's Word and filled with the Holy Spirit, Satan will destroy us. It was no coincidence that Judas was the keeper of the money. Jesus warns us over and over again in the gospels about the problem with money. Many followers of Messiah have sold Him out, just like Judas did. All ministers and lay people need to beware, for what may seem like a blessing may turn into a curse. And Satan is the great liar; after it is over, we will hate ourselves, just like Judas did. There is no theology that can properly explain it. We must understand that even after we are born again, we still are in this sinful body. Our lives can be used in God's service, or they can be used in Satan's. We all have those weak areas of our lives, and we must keep our sins confessed, and try not to put ourselves in a tempting situation.

It's one thing to start out in the race for the Messiah's kingdom; it's quite another to finish the race. This life is filled with detour signs and booby traps, and they all look enticing. We must keep our minds fixed on the narrow way, and not follow the crowd. We also need to be sensitive to the Holy Spirit, and discern when an opportunity is of God, or when it is a scheme of the devil.

THE LAST
PASSOVER

1) THE PREPARATION OF THE PASSOVER

Matthew 26:17–19, Mark 14:12–16, Luke 22:7–13: It was the first day of the Feast of Unleavened Bread, when the Passover lamb would be killed. Little did the disciples know *at this point,* that the "true Passover Lamb," Yeshua, would be killed. Jesus told them to go into Jerusalem, and they would meet a man carrying a pitcher of water. Normally, the women carried the water. The man took them to a large upper room, and the disciples made ready the Passover meal. Jesus, being God, had the *right* man, at the *right* time, to take them to the *right* place.

2) THE LAST PASSOVER

Matthew 26:20–29, Mark 14:22–25, Luke 22:14–20: The Feast of Passover was celebrated over 3,500 years ago down in the land of Egypt, when God delivered the Israelites out of Egyptian bondage. The feast was held on the 14th day of Nisan (March–April) each year. The entire Passover revolves around "the lamb" that is to be offered.

Exodus 12:6, Leviticus 23:5, Numbers 9:3, 28:16: A lamb, without spot or blemish, was to be slain and the blood placed on each side of the doorposts and over the door. When the death angel came through the land of Egypt, the firstborn in that house would be spared. This became the most important feast of the Jewish year, and forever changed their calendar. The lamb that was slain was a type of the Lamb of God, that would be slain one day for the sins of the world. This feast was observed strongly during the time of Yeshua, and He kept the last Passover with His disciples, before His death would fulfill the Jewish feast. Jesus said in Luke 22:15, "With *desire* I have desired to eat this passover with you before I suffer." In other words, the Messiah had a great *desire* to eat the Passover meal with His disciples before He *became the Passover!*

3) THE MEANING OF THE LORD'S SUPPER

When evening was come, Jesus sat down with the disciples. He took the bread and blessed it, and broke it, and gave it to the disciples, and said, "Take, eat; this is my body." So the bread, *matzah,* "unleavened bread," was a picture of His body. The prayer Jesus would have prayed over the bread was, "Blessed are you O Lord our God, King of the Universe, that bringeth forth bread from the earth." Jesus the Messiah was the Bread of Life, and He would be brought forth from the earth after He was buried. Then Jesus took the cup, "the cup of redemption," and gave thanks, and gave it to them, saying, "Drink ye all of it: For this is my blood of the *new testament,* (or

new *covenant*) which is shed for many for the remission of sins. But I say unto you, I will not drink henceforth of this fruit of the vine, until the day when I drink it new with you in my Father's kingdom." The "cup" was a symbol of His approaching death (Matt. 20:22; John 18:11). The "wine" was a symbol of His blood, that He would shed for the sins of the world. In John 6:54, Jesus said we must eat of His flesh, and drink of His blood to have everlasting life. This was a spiritual way of speaking about the ones who would trust in Him by faith. The Lord also mentions another "cup," "the cup of acceptance," that He would drink with his disciples in the future kingdom. When Israel accepts Jesus as the Messiah, then the thousand-year reign of Messiah will be set up on earth.

There are four crucial covenants, that all believers need to know:

1) THE ABRAHAMIC COVENANT
Genesis 15:18, 22:18: All the world would be blessed through the promise that God gave to Abraham. This was a permanent, unconditional covenant.

2) THE MOSAIC COVENANT
Deuteronomy 5:1–3: This covenant was a *temporary* covenant that God gave to the children of Israel when they were becoming a nation. They had to have civil, moral, and religious laws to live by. This covenant was conditional. If they obeyed, they would be blessed; if they disobeyed, they would be cursed.

3) THE DAVIDIC COVENANT
2 Samuel 7:16: God promised David that his kingdom would never end, and that from his seed would come a king that would sit on his throne forever.

4) THE NEW COVENANT
Hebrews 8:8: This is the covenant that Jesus the Messiah was talking about in the gospels. This covenant superseded the Mosaic Covenant. (The Abrahamic Covenant, and the Davidic Covenant, are still in effect.)

Only the Mosaic Covenant has been nullified. Let me give you an example: All the blessings that the world has enjoyed, especially we as believers, are a result of the Abrahamic Covenant (Gal. 3). The Messiah will return soon to fulfill the Davidic Covenant, and sit on the throne in Jerusalem (Matt. 19:28). But we are not bound to the Mosaic law, such as keeping the Sabbath Day, offering up animal sacrifices, tithing, etc. There has been so much error in the modern-day church over the years by not understanding these truths. It's good for us to honor the *Sabbath Day*, which was Saturday in the Bible, but let's not try to place people under bondage if they do not. We don't have to offer up *sacrifices* at the temple in Jerusalem anymore; the temple was destroyed in A.D. 70, and Jesus was the final sacrifice for all the sins of the world. We are to be generous with our *giving*, but not by compulsion or because some preacher is making us give a tithe to his church. These are just a few examples to show that we are not under the Mosaic Covenant any longer (Heb. 8:13). This is religious bondage, and millions are living under bondage in our world. We have been redeemed by the Messiah. His blood has set us free. We have been made righteous through our faith in Him. Jesus fulfilled the Law, something we could never do! (John 1:17).

However, there are many who say that all of the Old Testament has been done away with, and that it was all just history. My friends, just because we are not under the Mosaic law does not mean that the rest of the Old Testament is void and nullified. There are thousands of principles and truths in the Old Testament that are still relevant for us today. Listen to what Paul told Timothy in 2 Timothy 3:16, "All scripture is given by inspiration of God, and is profitable for doctrine, for reproof, for correction, for instruction in righteousness: That the man of God may be perfect, thoroughly furnished unto all good works." At the time of Paul's statement, he was mainly speaking of the Old Testament. This is why it is so crucial for us to "rightly *"divide"* the word of truth" (2 Tim. 2:15).

Jesus Washed the Disciples' Feet

John 13:1–17   The supper had ended. Jesus got up and laid aside His garments, took a towel and girded himself. He poured water into a basin and began washing the disciples' feet, and wiping them off with the towel that he had girded himself with. *What a picture!* The Son of God, washing dirt off of other men's feet, and then taking the towel from around His precious, sinless body, and wiping the feet dry.

After Simon Peter refused to let Jesus wash his feet, Jesus said to him, "If I wash thee not, thou hast no part with me." Then listen to what Peter said, "Lord, not my feet only, but also my hands and my head." Jesus saith unto him, "He that is washed needeth not save to wash his feet, but is clean *every whit*: and ye are clean, but not all."

What does this mean? In the days of Jesus, people walked on dusty roads, in sandals, and when they arrived at a house there would be a basin full of water to wash off the dirt from their feet. Their bodies didn't need washing, but their feet did. Likewise, when a person comes to the Messiah, His blood cleanses them of *all* their sin, but they still need cleansing of their daily sins, to stay in fellowship with the Father. When Jesus said, "but not all," He was speaking of Judas Iscariot, who would betray Him.

Jesus told the disciples that if He, being Master and Lord, would wash their feet, how much more should they wash one another's feet. He said, "Verily, verily, I say unto you, The servant is not greater than his lord; neither he that is sent greater than he that sent him."

I believe there is a more spiritual lesson here than the physical washing of someone's feet. Some religious groups still wash one another's feet at certain times, and I am not criticizing them. But the main message here is one of servanthood. We should serve each other, restore each other when one falls. The amazing thing about serving others is that, "If ye know these things, happy are ye if ye do them." The word "happy" is *makarios*, "supremely blessed." If we want to be blessed spiritually, we need to serve each other.

JOHN 14

John 14:1-31 This would have to be one of my personal favorite chapters in the Bible. Jesus has just finished eating the Passover meal with His disciples. He has washed their feet, and now He gives them words that will be a major part of their lives, and our lives, forever. Let's break it down in sections so we can understand better what He is saying.

Verses 1–6, Jesus foretells His coming: I memorized this passage many years ago, but it still brings a fresh joy to my heart, and I learn something new from it all the time. The disciples had left everything to follow Jesus of Nazareth, and now He is telling them that He is going to be killed. Their world is falling apart, and their hearts are about to shake out of their chests. They have been with Jesus throughout His ministry, seen all of those beautiful miracles, heard all of those wonderful sermons. They have seen the crowds shout praises to Jesus, but they have also seen the corrupt religious establishment try to kill Him. As they are gathered with Jesus in this upper room, their tension is great, their eyes are filled with questions. What are they supposed to do when Jesus leaves them? Here Jesus gives probably the most comforting words that were ever spoken: "Let not your heart be troubled; ye believe in God, believe also in me. In my Father's house are many mansions; if it were not so, I would have told you. I go to prepare a place for you. And if I go and prepare a place for you, I will come again, and receive you unto myself; that where I am, there ye may be also. And whither I go ye know, and the way ye know. Thomas saith unto him, Lord, we know not whither thou goest; and how can we know the way?

The Christ:

Jesus saith unto him, I am the way, the truth, and the life; no man cometh unto the Father but by me." Jesus takes them back to the very fundamental truths of the Christian faith. Do you believe in God? If you do, then I am God, in the form of a man. There really are many rooms in My Father's house, and I am going to prepare a place for you. If there were no heaven, I would tell you, but there is. I am going away, but I will be coming back to receive you to myself, so you can be with Me. There is *only one way* to the Father, and that is through Me! Jesus is not *a* way, He is *the* way! He did not say that He would *show* them the way, He said, I *am* the way! There are many denominations, many religious groups that man has started over the centuries, but there is *only one way* to heaven, through the Messiah, Jesus! We can learn *some* truth from going to church and reading books about Jesus, but He is the only *real* truth! Jesus will give us truths that no one else has the ability to give us. Jesus is called "the eternal life" in the Scriptures. He not only gives us life, *He is life!* In Hebrew, here is how Jesus would have said the last statement: *"Anee hahderech hah emet veh hah cha yeem."* I am the way, the truth, and the life.

A Jewish wedding: A man would go to the father of a young Jewish girl, and pay a price for his daughter. He would then offer her a cup of wine as a proposal. If she drank the wine, this was a sign that she had accepted his offer. He would then go back to the Jewish community where he lived, and add a room onto his father's house, just for his bride. It might take a year or more to build, but the bride knew that her bridegroom would be returning. It was her job to keep herself ready, and to keep an olive oil lamp burning brightly in her window, for she didn't know the day nor the hour when he would return. It was customary for the man to go get his bride at midnight, which made it more romantic. A host of friends would accompany them, and they would have a huge wedding reception. They would go back to the room that he had prepared at his father's house. We can see the close similarities of a Jewish wedding to the sermon Jesus gave to His disciples.

It has always been a great comfort to me to know that if there were no heaven, Jesus would have not come to this earth. Why did He suffer and die, and rise again, if there were no eternity? One day the Messiah will return for His bride, the Church, and the Church is made up of Jews and Gentiles who believe in Him.

Verses 7–12, "He that hath seen me hath seen the Father": What a statement! *Jesus is claiming to be God!* He was answering Philip's question, "Lord, show us the Father, and it sufficeth us." Jesus told them also to believe in Him, if nothing else, because of the works that He had done. And He says something that is very strange: "Verily, verily, I say unto you, He that believeth on me, the works that I do shall he do also: and greater works than these shall he do: because I go to my Father." This verse has caused a tremendous amount of arguments over the years. Was Jesus saying that all who believe in Him could raise the dead? Could they heal the blind? Could they walk on water? This is where I must say that we must rightly divide the Word of truth. The disciples who walked with Jesus would be able to perform miracles, in order to carry the message of the Messiah into all the world for the first time. Because Jesus was going to send the power of the Holy Spirit upon them, they would see *more* people come to know Jesus as the Messiah. Jesus only ministered for about three years on earth, and covered less than one hundred miles. They would carry the gospel into all the world, and leave behind the wonderful gospel narratives that we are still enjoying today. Although I still believe in divine healing, and we miss mighty miracles of God because of our unbelief, I do believe that most of the supernatural gifts were fulfilled in the Apostles. We don't have anyone today who can go to a funeral home and raise the dead! This is why we have so many different views about the Scriptures. There are different dispensations recorded in the Bible, and if one chooses not to believe in dispensations, they can take the Bible out of it's context and try to make it say something that it doesn't say.

Verses 13–15, The promise of answered prayer: Jesus gives the disciples a promise, that whatsoever they ask in His name will be done. The key is, the prayer must be offered up with praise to God, and all for the name of Yeshua to be glorified. It can't be just saying the name of "Jesus," but praying that His name will be exalted. Are we asking for something that will bring glory to God? Are we really praying for God's will to be done? Our prayers being answered depends completely on the fact that

Jesus the Messiah died and rose again. His *blood* has opened up a new way for us to pray, and God will hear our prayers! (Heb. 10:19–20).

Verses 16–26, The promise of the Holy Spirit: Jesus gives them the promise of the Holy Spirit, *Ruach Haqodesh.* The Holy Spirit would live inside of them, to comfort them, to give them wisdom, to teach them how to pray, to keep them from sinning. As they kept God's commandments, the Holy Spirit would abide with them. Their love for Jesus would be seen in their holy lives. "He shall teach you all things, and bring all things to your remembrance, whatsoever I have said unto you." Have you ever wondered how the disciples wrote the gospel accounts? They certainly could not have remembered all the things that Jesus said and did. They were so confused many times, they didn't even know the meaning of what Jesus was doing. When the *Ruach Haqodesh* came, He would bring to their remembrance all the things that Jesus said and did. This is why we read verses like John 2:22: "When therefore he was risen from the dead, his disciples *remembered* that he had said this unto them." We see here the work of the *Father* sending the *Son* into the world to die and rise again, and the *Holy Spirit* coming into the hearts of His people.

Verses 27–31, The promise of peace: Jesus was going to leave the disciples His peace, *shalom.* Shalom, in Hebrew, has a much deeper meaning than the English word "peace." We have a kind of peace when our circumstances are good, the family is doing good, and our finances are good. If we live in a nice home, have a good paying job, and our health is good, there is a peace that comes from that. And certainly this is not a sinful peace, but it is not what Jesus was talking about. Shalom carries a deeper meaning than the Greek word *eirene.* When all of the world would come against these disciples, they would have the "peace of God" that passes all understanding. Their peace would not hinge on their circumstances, or their earthly conditions. This is the peace that we all need, the peace that the Messiah left His disciples. They would all die for the gospel; only John would die a natural death. What would make these men give their lives for a cause, if it were not real? They were troubled when Jesus spoke these words to them, but later they would enjoy His shalom!

I AM
THE VINE

John 15:1–11   After the Upper Room discourse, Jesus and His disciples were walking away from Jerusalem, eastward. These words were spoken on their way to the garden of Gethsemane. *"Anee hah gefen hah a mee teet,"* "I am the true Vine, and my Father is the husbandman. Every branch in me that beareth not fruit he *taketh away*; and every branch that beareth fruit, he purgeth it, that it may bring forth more fruit." This is another one of the great, *"I Am"* sayings of Jesus, which showed His deity. This was the name used for God in the Old Testament (Exod. 3:14).

The words "taketh away," in Greek, *airos*, means "to lift up, or take away." The translators in 1611 thought it meant "taketh away," but a proper understanding of the culture during the time of Jesus will help us here. Many of the grape vines in Israel laid on the ground. As the branch grew away from the vine, it would eventually grow back into the ground, therefore killing the entire vine. They would place rocks underneath the branches to lift them up, so they would not grow into the ground. This would allow the branches to keep bearing grapes. What Jesus was saying was, when you are not bearing fruit for me, I will "lift you up," *airos*, so you will bear fruit. This is one of the many examples in the Scriptures where we cannot build a doctrine based on the English translation.

When we are bearing fruit for Jesus, sometimes we need pruning so we will bear more fruit. We cannot bring forth fruit unless we abide in Him. As we stay in His Word, His Word cleans us up day by day. If a man is not in Christ, he will be cast away. It brings glory to the Father when we bear fruit. So what is fruit? Some people think if they live a clean, good, moral life, they are bearing fruit. But the Pharisees were clean outwardly, and wicked inwardly. Spiritual fruit is "love, joy, peace, longsuffering, gentleness, goodness, faith, meekness, temperance" (Gal.5:22–23). There's a big difference in just being a good, moral person and bearing spiritual fruit for the Messiah.

Jesus tells them in verses 9–14 to continue in His love. They are to love one another, as He has loved them. Jesus would prove His great love by giving His life for His friends. The reason Jesus spoke these words to them, about abiding in His Word, was so their joy would be full. When people are abiding in Jesus, and loving each other, there is no greater joy on earth!

Jesus and His Friends

John 15:15–27   There is a progressive intimacy in John's Gospel. They were called "servants" in John 13:16; here they are called "friends" in verse 15. These disciples had been with Jesus from the beginning of His earthly ministry (verse 27), and He had chosen them (verse 16) to go into the world, and bring forth spiritual fruit. They would have the power of the Holy Spirit (verse 26) to help them, and their prayers would be answered (verse 16).

They were not to be discouraged because the world hated them; the world hated Jesus, too. They were not to be friends with the world, but friends of Jesus. The Messiah suffered, and they would suffer, too. The world would have no excuse for their sin (verse 22), because the works that Jesus had done, *had never been done by any other man* (verse 24). All of this happened, in order that the Scriptures might be fulfilled. "They hated me without a cause" (Ps. 35:19, 69:4). Are we a friend of the world, or are we a friend of Jesus? We are His friends *if* we do what He has commanded. *If* we love Him, *if* we love each other, *if* we stay in His Word, then we are His friends.

THE TIME IS
GETTING CLOSER

John 16:1–33 Jesus, knowing that His time on earth was drawing to an end, wanted to give the disciples some warnings about what to expect in the near future. He tells them not to be offended (verse 1), that the synagogues would cast them out (verse 2) because those in the synagogues do not know the Father (verse 3). Jesus did not tell them about all of this at the beginning, because He was still with them (verse 4), but now He is about to go away (verse 5).

Verses 6–11: He tells them not to be sorrowful, He must go away, so the Holy Spirit will come. There will be a great work done by the Holy Spirit. He will reprove the world of sin and of righteousness and of judgment.

Verses 12–15: At this point, the disciples could not bear all the things that Jesus wanted to say. Later, when the Spirit of truth came, He would give them the whole picture. This is a pre-authentication of the New Testament we have today. Later, the disciples would fully understand all the things Jesus said, and they would, through the help of the Holy Spirit, take the gospel into the world and leave the written Scriptures behind. Just think of all of the beautiful writings of James, Peter, and John, that would be written years later.

Verses 16–33: One of the key verses is, "Verily, verily, I say unto you, That ye shall weep and lament, but the world shall rejoice; and ye shall be sorrowful, but your sorrow shall be turned to joy." Jesus was speaking of His death and Resurrection. The disciples would see the

Messiah die on a tree, but they would see Him after He arose from the grave. Jesus came into the world that He created, and now He was about to go back to the Father (verse 28). The disciples now realized that Jesus was no longer speaking in proverbs (verses 25 and 29), but that He was speaking plainly. Jesus tells them they will be scattered (verse 32) and He will be left alone, but He is not alone, because the Father is with Him. A wonderful promise Jesus gives in verse 33, "These things I have spoken unto you, that in me ye might have peace. In the world ye shall have tribulation: but be of good cheer: I have overcome the world."

Jesus tells them they will suffer in the world, but He tells them they have nothing to fear, He will conquer the world. If we as believers could just grasp this wonderful truth, we would not live such defeated lives!

THE MESSIAH'S PRAYER

John 17:1–26   We have been trained to bow our heads and close our eyes when we pray. But when the Messiah prayed, He lifted up His eyes to heaven. This chapter is filled with profound truths that can help all of us. Try to imagine Jesus in the garden of Gethsemane, talking to the Father. We will break it down into *eight* petitions:

1) *Glorify thy Son, that thy Son may glorify thee* — Jesus, the Son of God, prays to God the Father, and acknowledges the power He was given over all flesh, and that He should give eternal life to as many as the Father has given Him. Eternal life is knowing God, through Jesus Christ, the One the Father sent into the world. The Son has glorified the Father while on earth (verses 1–4).

2) *Restore His eternal glory* — The Son was with the Father before the world was ever created, and He laid down His eternal glory to become a man. Here Jesus is praying for that eternal glory to be restored. After His death and Resurrection, He will ascend back to the Father (verse 5).

3) *The safety of the believers from the world* — The disciples were safe as long as Jesus was in the world, but now He is going away. He is praying for the Father to keep them safe after He goes back to heaven (verse 11).

4) *The safety of the believers from Satan* — Jesus knew that Satan would try to destroy His disciples, and He prays for the Father to keep them from evil (verse 15).

5) *The sanctification of the believers* — Jesus is praying for the Father to keep them in His Word, and set them apart as holy men of God. The truths of God would sanctify them (verse 17).

6) *The spiritual unity of the believers* — Jesus knew that some of the disciples were from different backgrounds. Peter was a fisherman, Matthew was a tax-collector, etc. They had already disputed who would be the greatest in the kingdom. Here, Jesus is praying to the Father for them to have a unity of spirit (verses 11, 21, and 22).

7) *That the world may believe* — The disciples needed to have unity of spirit, so that people in the world would believe in Jesus as the Messiah. Jesus is praying for the lost to be saved, who will hear the message of the disciples (verses 21 and 23).

8) *That the believers will be with Him in heaven, and behold His glory* — Jesus prayed for those that the Father had given Him to one day be with Him in glory. Eternal security of the believer is not based on the believer's ability to live good enough, but on the Father's answer to His Son's prayer. The ultimate goal is that one day we, as followers of the Messiah, will see His glory, and be where He is! (verse 24).

How privileged these disciples were, to have been chosen to be the ones to walk with Jesus and be His messengers. After Jesus left this earth, and the Holy Spirit came, they would know that *truly* Jesus did come forth from God (John 16:30, 17:8, 25). They were faithful to proclaim His message, and that is how the gospel of the Messiah has stood the test of time. *It was a historical fact!*

THE MESSIAH'S AGONY

Matthew 26:30–46
Mark 14:26–42
Luke 22:39–46
John 18:1

It is getting late in the night, and Jesus and His disciples are walking into the Garden of Gethsemane. They sang a hymn, which is believed to be Psalm 118, and, if this is true, one of the verses is Psalm 118:22: "The stone which the builders refused has become the head stone of the corner." What a timely hymn to sing, as the Messiah is the stone that the builders rejected, and He is the chief cornerstone. He is about to become that chief cornerstone.

Jesus quotes from Zechariah 13:7, "I will smite the shepherd, and the sheep of the flock shall be scattered abroad." This verse will be fulfilled when the Messiah is crucified, and all of the disciples flee. Jesus then tells them, "But after I am risen again, I will go before you into Galilee." This is a beautiful thing that Jesus says here. He met the disciples, and called them, by the Sea of Galilee, and they have been with Him for three years in His ministry. Now He wants them to know that after all of this dying business is over, He will rise again, and meet them. Where? Galilee — back in the place where he called them. We shall look at this when we get to John 21.

Jesus comes to Gethsemane *(oil press),* where He prays in such agony that His sweat is like great drops of blood. All the weight of the sins of the world are *pressing* upon Jesus. With James, Peter, and John falling asleep, because it is nigh unto midnight, Jesus falls on His face and prays, "O my Father, if it be possible, let this cup pass from me:

nevertheless not as I will, but as thou wilt." Here we can see the humanity of Yeshua, surrendering as a man, to do the Father's will. This is really where the battle was won. In Mark 14:35, Jesus prays that if it were possible, the hour might pass from Him. There was no other way for the sin of the world to be paid in full. Yeshua was God, but He was also man, in order to even be capable of dying. If man could have been justified by keeping the Law, or by religious deeds, then there would have been some other way.

When we travel to Israel, we always go to the Garden of Gethsemane where there are about eight olive trees, whose roots date back to the time of Jesus. All of the trees were cut down by the Romans in A.D. 70. There is a church there called the "Church of all Nations," where inside is a huge rock that is believed to be the rock where Jesus knelt and prayed. I was there one time when there were no tourists, and they allowed us to walk inside the iron fence and touch the stone. It was an awesome experience to think that the Messiah may have

prayed on that very rock. But it's not the rock where He prayed that is so important, it is the fact that our Lord Jesus loved us enough to give himself on our behalf. In the Garden is where it happened. He could have walked up over the Mount of Olives and, in just a little while, been safe in the Judean wilderness. He knew what was going to happen, but this was His main mission. He came to earth, born of a virgin, supernaturally, but He would die the death of a criminal, on a tree, in a very humiliating way. The Scriptures must be fulfilled. *The hour had come.* Judas and the band of soldiers were on their way.

THE ARREST OF
THE MESSIAH

Matthew 26:47–56
Mark 14:43–51
Luke 22:47–53
John 18:2–11

As we read the four Gospel accounts, we find several very touching incidents in the arrest of the Messiah. First of all, Yeshua knew where Judas could easily find Him. He had been with the disciples there on many occasions. He made it very easy for them to arrest Him. Second, the Jewish Feast of Passover had arrived, and all the things concerning the Messiah's first coming had to fulfill the Hebrew Scriptures. It is very moving for me to read about a multitude of soldiers, along with the chief priests and Pharisees, with Judas leading the way, coming in the night to arrest the Son of God. They carried lanterns, torches, and weapons. But this night, they would not need their weapons, only a kiss from the Satan-filled Judas.

According to Matthew's account, when Judas came to Jesus, Jesus called him "Friend." Jesus did not disown Judas, even in his betrayal. In John 13:21–30, when Jesus told the disciples that one of them would betray Him, Peter was reclining across the table, John was reclining to the left of Jesus, and Judas was on the right of Jesus. Peter told John to ask Him who it was that should betray Him. John leaned backward on the bosom of the Son of God, and said, "Lord, who is it?" Jesus said it was the one to whom He would give the sop, or bread, which was a sign of *friendship*. When Jesus gave the sop to Judas, Judas left, and went out, and it was *night*.

So here at the arrest, we can see the darkness that filled Judas's heart. It was night when they came to arrest Jesus, and it was *night* in the heart of one of His disciples.

Jesus knew all the things that were to happen, so He said to the band, "Whom seek ye? They answered Him, "Jesus of Nazareth."

"Jesus saith unto them, *I Am*, and they went backward to the ground." In the original transcripts, the word "he" is not there. Jesus said the same words that God spoke to Moses — *"I Am."* Just the mention of the name of God caused the multitude to fall to the ground. It is amazing that they were allowed the power to arrest the Lord God Almighty with a few weapons.

Peter drew out a sword and cut off the right ear of one of the servants of the high priest, a man named Malchus, *Melekh*, which means "king." Little did this servant "king" know that he had come to arrest the real servant, *the King of kings and Lord of lords.* Jesus reached out and healed the servant's ear. Even when people hated Him, Jesus showed compassion. What a Savior!

In Matthew 26:53–54, we find some powerful words of Jesus: "Thinkest thou that I cannot now pray to my Father, and he shall presently give me more than twelve legions of angels? But how then shall the scriptures be fulfilled, that thus it must be?" A legion of Roman soldiers was 6,000 men. More than 12 legions would be more than 72,000 angels. One angel destroyed 185,000 men in the Old Testament. Try to imagine how powerful 72,000 would be. The Messiah could have called for over 72,000 angels to come to His rescue, but all the Scriptures had to be fulfilled. If the disciples had been able to have fought the mob, and won, the Scriptures would *not* have been fulfilled. Jesus was in the temple many times, and they could not arrest Him, because the time was not right. But here, the time was right, things were going as planned, the Messiah knew what things were about to take place, and He would spend a long night before the religious leaders. So, "they led Him away."

THE TRIAL OF
THE MESSIAH

Matthew 26:57–68, 27:1
Mark 14:53–65
Luke 22:54, 63–71
John 18:12–14, 19–24 It is very important here, that we study
Psalm 22 and Isaiah 53. We can see the prophecies unfolding about
the Messiah being despised and rejected, and being accused by false
witnesses. We can also see the prophecy of the Messiah *"opening not
his mouth"* as He held His peace before the high priest.

From the Garden of Gethsemane, they took Jesus across the
Kidron valley to the house of the high priest, Caiaphas, *Kayafa*. I have
been in the dungeon where many scholars believe they kept Jesus that
night. The cold and damp feeling I got reminded me that Jesus went
through all the cold and lonely feelings that we could possibly feel
when death comes to us. We never have to worry about being alone
when it comes our time to die. Jesus has already been there!

It was late at *night* when they took Jesus away to the high priest,
which was against Jewish law. The arrest was through the agency
of a *traitor*, which was also in violation of the Mosaic law (Lev.
19:16–18). The Messiah was judged in *private*, which was against
Jewish law (Deut. 19:16–18). The *indictment* against Jesus was illegal, because it was vague and indefinite (Deut. 17:2–6, 19:15).
The *proceedings* were illegal, because they were held on the eve of
the Passover, and the day preceding a Jewish Sabbath. According to
Leviticus 21:10, it was not lawful for a priest to *rend his garment*,
but Caiaphas did. The Sanhedrin violated Jewish law when they *spit
in His face and struck Him.*

The religious leaders were motivated by their jealousy against Jesus. When they saw that Jesus could heal the incurable, when they saw Him overturn the moneychangers, and when they saw Him raise Lazarus from the dead, their hearts were filled with hatred. This proves that miracles do not make people believe in Jesus as the Messiah. They saw many of the miracles, but they refused to believe in Yeshua as their Messiah.

It's hard for us to understand how these leaders could have been so blind, with Jesus standing in their midst. They thought they were placing Jesus on trial, when in reality, they were the ones on trial, and they didn't even know it.

THE DENIAL OF PETER

Matthew 26:69–75
Mark 14:66–72
Luke 22:55–62
John 18:15–18, 25–27 Jesus made the prediction back in John 13:36–38 that Peter would deny Him three times. Peter followed afar off when they led Jesus away, even to the palace, and warmed himself *"beside a fire."* A maid recognized Peter, because his speech gave him away: "For thou art a Galilaean, and thy speech agreeth thereto" (Mark 14:70).

Cocks were not allowed in Jerusalem during the feasts, but cocks were in the castle of Antonio, on the northwest corner of the temple, where the Roman soldiers were. The term "cock crowing" was used for the third watch of the night (Mark 13:35). At each "cock crowing," the Roman relieved a guard that was on duty. Peter denied Jesus three times, and it was three hours after midnight, then he went out and wept bitterly.

Did Peter really believe that Yeshua was the Messiah? Why is this dark moment in Peter's life recorded? Yes, Peter knew Yeshua was the Messiah, and he loved Him greatly. Jesus knew that Peter was going to deny Him, but it was all needed to sift Peter. It is recorded to show all of us that no matter how spiritual we think we are, we can still fail our Lord. Haven't we all denied our Lord at certain times? This was all part of making Peter the great man that he would one day become. God uses even our failures in life to make us the followers we need to be. The weeping of Peter after this denial was part of breaking him from being too prideful again.

Peter did not realize three things:

1) his weakness
2) his pride
3) the love of the Messiah

God sees our weaknesses, our pride, and our lack of understanding of who He is. That's why He sent Yeshua into the world.

We shall see later, where the Messiah will talk to Peter again, "beside a fire."

To Pilate, to Herod, Back to Pilate

Matthew 27:2, 11–14
Mark 15:1–5
Luke 23:1–16
John 18:28–38, 19:1, 4–15

Here we can see how God sent the Messiah into the world *"in the fullness of time."* The Jewish way to kill someone was by stoning, but the Romans crucified their victims. God was using the powers that be to fulfill the Hebrew Scriptures: "Jesus answered, Thou couldest have no power at all against me, except it were given thee from above" (John 19:11).

Pontius Pilate was the procurator of Jerusalem. Herod Antipas was the ruler over the territory of Galilee and Perea. When Jesus was taken to Pilate, it was early in the morning (John 18:28), about six o'clock. Pilate had been given orders by Caesar to stop any Messianic revolts by the Jews. If he could not keep down trouble, he would lose his job. But there was a problem: *"He could find no fault in Jesus."* So when Pilate realized that Jesus was from Galilee, he thought quickly how to get free of this disturbing Jesus of Nazareth. He would send him to Herod, who was in Jerusalem also, during the Feast of Passover, to make sure the Jews were kept under control (Luke 23:6–7). Interestingly enough, Herod was glad to see Jesus, because he had heard of Him and wanted to see Him perform a miracle. Yeshua had traveled all around Galilee in His earthly ministry, but stayed away from Tiberias, the city of Herod. Now, they meet face to face, and what does Herod find? The same thing Pilate found: "no fault in Him." The Jews always examined their Passover lambs *the night before* the feast, and here, *the night before*, the true Passover Lamb was examined.

Herod mocked Jesus, placed a gorgeous robe on Him, and sent Him back to Pilate. Pilate and Herod were enemies before this day, but now they became friends (Luke 23:12). It's amazing how even the world's most wicked men will join hands against their Creator.

When Pilate saw that Jesus had been sent back to him, he told the religious leaders that neither he nor Herod had found any fault in this man. Pilate said, "I will therefore chastise him, and release him." Here we will read Luke 23:17–19: "(For of necessity he must release one unto them at the feast.) And they cried out all at once, saying, Away with this man, and release unto us Barabbas: (Who for certain sedition made in the city, and for murder, was cast into prison.)" The name Barabbas, *Bar-Ab-ba*, means "son of the father." Barabbas was loosed from the prison house and was allowed to live, all because the "Son of the Father" died in his stead. No matter how vile a person may be, through faith in the Messiah, one can be set free from the prison house of sin!

THE MOCKING AND SCOURGING BY THE ROMAN SOLDIERS

Matthew 27:27–32
Mark 15:16–21
Luke 23:26
John 19:2–3

We can see the fulfillment of Psalm 22:7–8. The Mel Gibson movie *The Passion of the Christ* has received a tremendous amount of attention. (I rejoice in the truths that are presented in that movie, and that even Hollywood is preaching the gospel!) Mel Gibson showed the scourging of the Messiah to be extreme, and we know from Isaiah's prophecy in 52:14 that He was beaten beyond recognition. However, the fact that the Gospel writers do not go into detail about the intensity of the beating should tell us that the focus of their accounts was not so much about what the antagonists did to Jesus, but the fact that *He gave himself for all of us!*

They placed a crown of thorns on His head, which reminds me of what happened after the fall in Genesis 3:17–18: "Cursed is the ground for thy sake; in sorrow shalt thou eat of it all the days of thy life: Thorns also and thistles shall it bring forth to thee." The result of sin's fall brought forth *thorns,* and it was a *crown of thorns* that was placed on the precious head of Jesus.

They placed a purple robe on Jesus and mocked Him saying, "Hail, King of the Jews!" Then, they took the purple robe off of Him, placed His own robe upon Him, and led Him away to be crucified. They found a man of Cyrene, Simon, *Shimon,* to carry the execution stake. I believe this man was the most blessed man who ever lived. Try to imagine the feeling of being the one chosen to carry the cross of Jesus. This would stay with Simon all the days of his life, and history reveals that he became a sincere follower of the Messiah, and was the father of Alexander and Rufus, who also were followers of Jesus (Mark 15:21).

He had traveled a long way coming to the Jewish Passover, not knowing what was going to happen. Historians believe that he was a black, Jewish man, who was part of the *diaspora*, or dispersion. He carried the crossbeam, that held the precious hands of Yeshua. It would not be nails that would hold those hands, but His eternal love for human beings, one of which was Simon of Cyrene.

THE CRUCIFIXION
OF THE MESSIAH

Matthew 27:33–56
Mark 15:22–41
Luke 23:27–49
John 19:16–30

It was prophesied that the Messiah would be crucified, in Psalm 22, Isaiah 53, and in the types and shadows of the Jewish law. These prophecies were 250 years *before* crucifixion was invented by Tarquin the Proud, a Phoenician, to the Roman world in the sixth century B.C. It would be one thousand years *before* the prophecies would be fulfilled. The accuracy of the Scriptures is phenomenal!

They led Jesus to a place called Golgotha, *Gulgota*, "the place of the skull." It was nigh unto the city of Jerusalem. There are two places in Jerusalem which scholars believe *could* be the place. One is within the Holy Sepulchre, where the Catholics commemorate the death of Jesus, and the other is Gordon's Calvary, on the north side of the city, where there is a hewn-out rock tomb and a beautiful garden. While both places can be convincing, in all probability the Holy Sepulchre may be the correct location, but it is much more moving to visit the Garden Tomb area. When we take our tours to Israel, this is certainly one of the highlights of the tour. But again, the exact spot is not important. God did not want us to worship the *place*, but the *person* of the Messiah!

It was the "third hour," nine o'clock in the morning, when Jesus was crucified. It has been commonly thought over the years that Jesus was crucified on a tall, square-timbered cross, on top of a hill. But in actuality it was the Roman custom to crucify their victims on level ground, so the people could walk by and laugh and jeer. Also, Jesus was close enough to the ground that He talked to John about taking care of His mother. They nailed the hands of Jesus to the crossbeam, and then nailed the crossbeam to an old olive tree, where a small platform was placed on the olive tree for the feet of Jesus to rest. This is how Satan would bruise His heel (Gen. 3:15). Jesus would push His body up in order to breathe. It was a very crude and bloody scene that day, with the naked, bruised body of Jesus hanging on a tree, with a crown of thorns on His head (Deut. 21:23; Gal. 3:13; 1 Pet. 2:24; Acts 5:30). Pilate wrote a title, and placed it on the cross: JESUS OF NAZARETH THE KING OF THE JEWS. It was written in Greek, Latin, and Hebrew. The Greek language was the common language of the Roman empire; Latin was the language of the Romans; Hebrew was the language of the religious Jews.

Once again, the Scriptures simply say "and they crucified him." The details are left out, but we know from archaeology finds and the writings of historians that it was a very humiliating way to die. The blood of the Messiah had to be *shed*; it could not remain in His body. The saved people would have to be *washed* in the blood of the Messiah!

Many of the people mocked him, the two thieves mocked him, and the religious leaders mocked him, saying, "He saved others: let him save himself, if he be the Christ, the chosen of God." The soldiers mocked him, offering him a sponge of vinegar that was placed on a reed. Every Roman soldier had his own sponge that they used for toilet purposes, for they did not have soft tissue in those days. They stuck the filthiest thing they had to the face of Jesus. We can see *how sinful* the world really is when we see the Cross. We can see *how serious* life really is when we see the Cross. Jesus would have never died on the Cross if there were no heaven or hell. Each class of people represented at the cross would find salvation. Many of the people who mocked Jesus were saved on the Day of Pentecost. One of the two thieves was saved just before Jesus died. Some of the priests were even saved in the first church at Jerusalem (Acts 6:7).

From the days when the Messiah was in Galilee, He told His disciples that He would be killed, and that on the third day He would rise again. This was His *main mission*. It was going to take *more* than a few sermons to save the world. It was going to take *more* than a few miracles to save the world. It was going to take the *death* of the Messiah to redeem a lost world!

WHO CRUCIFIED THE MESSIAH?

Acts 4:27   For of a truth against thy holy child Jesus, whom thou hast anointed, both Herod, and Pontius Pilate, with the Gentiles, and the people of Israel, were gathered together, For to do whatsoever thy hand and thy counsel determined before to be done."

The question needs to be asked, "Who crucified the Messiah?" Here we find the answer:

1) *Herod and Pontius Pilate* — They were the rulers in the days Jesus was crucified. So they are responsible.

2) *The Gentiles* — The Roman soldiers were responsible, for they were the ones who drove the nails into the hands and feet of Jesus.

3) *The people of Israel* — Not all of the common Jews, but the corrupt Jewish establishment. The religious leaders were responsible.

4) *God the Father* — "He that spared not His own Son, but delivered Him up for us all" (Rom. 8: 32). God was responsible.

5) *Jesus himself* — "No man taketh it from me, but I lay it down of myself" (John 10:18). Jesus was responsible — He gave himself.

6) *Everyone* — "For he hath made him to be sin for *us*, who knew no sin, that *we* might be made the righteousness of God in him" (2 Cor. 5:21). It was *our* sins that crucified Jesus.

There has been so much anti-Semitism over the centuries, even among the so-called Christians. Many of the early Catholics said that all of the Jews were Christ-killers. Many of the church reformers, like Luther and Calvin, said that all of the Jews were Christ-killers. This has also led to a tremendous error called "replacement theology" which says that God is through with the Jews, and all of the promises pertaining to Israel now belong to the Church. The truth is, thousands of the common people in Jesus' day loved Him, and who do you think carried the gospel into all of the world? Who were the people saved on the Day of Pentecost? Who were the disciples? Who was Jesus? They were all Jews! The Scriptures were written down by Jews. The Gentiles need to go back to the Scripture and find out where their salvation comes from. This is one reason the modern-day Church is not seeing real revival. We have turned the Scriptures into a Gentile, Western-world idea. Our Christian heritage is not from Rome or Greece, but Israel! Jesus was a Jew who died for Jews and Gentiles. I don't know about you, but I am so thankful that the Jewish Messiah included me in His plan!

THE PASSOVER LAMB

1) THE HEBREW PROPHECIES

Exodus 12:6   And ye shall keep it up until the fourteenth day of the same month; and the whole assembly of the congregation of Israel shall kill it *in the evening.*"

Exodus 12:13: ". . . and when I see the blood, I will pass over you,"

Exodus 12:46: ". . . neither shall ye break a bone thereof."

Isaiah 53:7: "He was oppressed, and he was afflicted, yet he opened not his mouth: he is brought as a lamb to the slaughter, and as a sheep before her shearers is dumb, so he openeth not his mouth."

Zechariah 12:10: ". . . and they shall look upon me whom they have pierced,"

Zechariah 13:6: "And one shall say unto him, What are these wounds in thine hands? Then he shall answer, Those with which I was wounded in the house of my friends."

2) THE HISTORICAL SITUATION

John 1:29   "Behold the Lamb of God, which taketh away the sin of the world."

Mark 15:34: "And at the *ninth hour* Jesus cried with a loud voice."

Mark 15:37: "And Jesus cried with a loud voice, and gave up the ghost."

John 19:32–37: "Then came the soldiers, and brake the legs of the first, and of the other which was crucified with him. But when they came to Jesus, and saw that he was dead already, they brake not his legs: But one of the soldiers with a spear pierced his side, and forthwith came there out blood and water. And he that saw it bare record, and his record is true: and he knoweth

that he saith true, that ye might believe. For these things were done, that the scripture should be fulfilled, *A bone of him shall not be broken*. And again another scripture saith, *They shall look on him whom they pierced.*"

The "ninth hour" was three o'clock in the afternoon. When the priest blew the shofar at three o'clock in the temple, signifying that the Passover lamb had been offered up on the altar, the true Passover Lamb, Yeshua the Messiah, died on the tree. The 14th day of Nisan, Friday afternoon, fulfilling the Feast of Passover. All of the types and shadows in the Old Testament concerning the death of the Messiah were fulfilled. Peter would later write in 1 Peter 1:19, "as of a lamb without blemish and without spot." John would later describe Jesus in Revelation 13:8 as "the Lamb slain from the foundation of the world."

3) THE SPIRITUAL APPLICATION

Revelation 1:5 Unto him that loved us, and washed us from our sins in his own blood."

Ephesians 2:13: "But now in Christ Jesus ye who sometimes were afar off are made nigh by the blood of Christ."

Hebrews 9:22: ". . . without shedding of blood, [there] is no remission [of sins]."

Have we accepted Yeshua as our Passover Lamb? Have we been washed in the blood of the Messiah? Have we been made righteous through faith in His blood? Do we believe the testimony of the disciples? Do we believe that Yeshua is the prophesied Messiah?

THE MIRACLES
AT THE CROSS

1) SUPERNATURAL DARKNESS

Matthew 27:45   Now from the sixth hour there was *darkness* over all the land unto the ninth hour." This fulfilled the passage in Amos 8:9: "And it shall come to pass in that day, saith the Lord GOD, that I will cause the sun to go down at noon, and I will darken the earth in the clear day." From twelve o'clock noon, until three o'clock in the afternoon there was darkness on the earth. This darkness was documented by Roman historians from the time of Jesus. The sun refused to shine, because the Son of God was dying. There was no light, because the Light of the World was dying.

The Messiah stepped into the darkness and defeated the powers of hell. Everything that would keep us from going to heaven was placed upon Jesus. The only perfect man, the God-man, Christ Jesus, was being crucified. God made the world, He became a man and came into His world, but the world didn't want Him. The darkest day the world has ever known was when the altogether lovely Lord Jesus was crucified.

2) THE VEIL OF THE TEMPLE WAS RENT

Matthew 27:51   And, behold, the veil of the temple was rent in twain from the top to the bottom." The veil was four inches thick, 30 feet wide, and 60 feet tall. Not even a team of oxen could have torn the veil, but God made two pieces out of it, beginning at the top, then down to the bottom. The veil was a type of the humanity of the Messiah. A new and living way had been opened to all who would trust in Yeshua as the Messiah (Heb. 10:20). The veil was made of purple, blue, and scarlet, with "cunning work" that was seen on both sides of the veil. It separated the "Holy of Holies" from "the Holy Place." It was only entered once a year, by the high priest, on Yom Kippur, the Day of Atonement. The true High Priest, *Yeshua ha Mashiach*, had made a way for those who believe to enter into heaven itself. No more need for the animal sacrifices — the Lamb of God had been offered up. He only had to die *one time*, and He will never have to die again. The Old Testament priests would die; Yeshua, our High Priest, will never die! A new dispensation had arrived — the dispensation of grace!

3) THERE WAS AN EARTHQUAKE, AND THE ROCKS RENT

Matthew 27:51 And the earth did quake, and the rocks rent." The Creator of the earth had died, and the earth expressed her grief. No one had ever died like Jesus before. There was a cross in the shadow of the manger in Bethlehem. He was born, not to live to be old, for He was older than eternity, but to give His life so we might live eternally. Without the Cross, there would be no salvation. Without the Cross, there would be no forgiveness. Until we have knelt at the Cross, all else is in vain. The earthquake should make all of us say exactly what the Roman centurion and the people who were with him said as they watched Jesus on the Cross, and saw the earthquake. They feared greatly, saying, "Truly this was the Son of God."

DEATH
DESTROYED DEATH

Exodus 7:10–12   And Moses and Aaron went in unto Pharaoh, and they did so as the LORD had commanded: and Aaron cast down his rod before Pharaoh, and before his servants, and it became a serpent. Then Pharaoh also called the wise men and the sorcerers: now the magicians of Egypt, they also did in like manner with their enchantments. For they cast down every man his rod, and they became serpents: but Aaron's rod swallowed up their rods."

The serpent here is a picture of Satan, who caused our first parents to sin in the Garden of Eden. God used a rod and turned it into a serpent in order to destroy the serpent. Listen to Hebrews 2:14, "Forasmuch then as the children are partakers of flesh and blood, he [Messiah] also himself likewise took part of the same; that through death he might destroy him that had the power of death, that is, the devil." As the serpents of Pharaoh were swallowed up by a serpent, Jesus willingly died, in order to destroy death. Sin was destroyed by the Messiah who became sin for us. "Death is swallowed up in victory" (Isa. 25:8; 1 Cor. 15:54).

Those verses in John 3:14–15, become more clear now, "And as Moses lifted up the serpent in the wilderness, even so must the Son of man be lifted up; That whosoever believeth in him should not perish, but have eternal life." We all have been bitten by the serpent, and the poison of sin is in our hearts. But God has provided the antidote — Yeshua the Messiah! If we will look to Him, we shall live!

Jesus came to take away the fear of death. One of the wonderful benefits of knowing Jesus as the Messiah is that He takes the terrible fear of death away. We still have the natural desire to live as long as we can, but we also know that physical death is coming to all of us. Until we are ready to die, we are not ready to live for Jesus.

So many professing Christians are looking for the material blessings of this temporary life, and when death comes knocking on their door, they fall all to pieces. So many just want to read about the miracles of Jesus, and they forget the real reason why He came. Have you ever wondered how the disciples could face death so bravely? They knew that Jesus conquered death, and He had promised them the same victory. Do you know today, that when you die, you will live again? Jesus died, so you can have that assurance! He has passed through the valley so we will not have to be afraid!

THE BURIAL
OF THE MESSIAH

Matthew 27:57–60
Mark 15:43–46
Luke 23:50–54
John 19:38–42

It was written in the Law, that if someone was defiled by a dead body, they were to keep the Passover Feast on the 14th day of the *second* month. This was called *Pesach Sheni*. This is a strange passage, but it was put there for a particular purpose. There would be two men who would need this law, and those two men were Joseph of Arimathea, *Yoseph of Ramatayim*, and Nicodemus, *Nakdimon*. According to John 19:31, it was "an high day," meaning the Passover Sabbath. The body of Jesus could not remain upon the cross on the Sabbath day.

Joseph was a disciple of Yeshua, and Nicodemus had no doubt been converted after his conversation with Yeshua back in John 3. Joseph went to Pontius Pilate and "craved" for the body of Jesus. This man really loved our Lord. Nicodemus came with about one hundred pounds of myrrh and aloes. They took the body of Jesus, wrapped it in new, fine linen cloth — no doubt Joseph bought the very best. They did "as the manner of the Jews was to bury," meaning they did *not* embalm like the Egyptians, they anointed the body with spices.

They brought the body of Jesus to a place where "there was a garden: and in the garden a new sepulchre, wherein was never man yet laid." I find it interesting and beautiful that the Messiah came into this world through a virgin girl *"who had never known a man."* Jesus rode a donkey into Jerusalem *"whereon never a man sat."* And He is laid in a tomb *"wherein was never man yet laid."* The Messiah Jesus was pure, sinless, and from heaven. He was treated as such by those who loved Him.

Do we "crave" the body of Jesus? How far would we go to be near Jesus? Joseph loved Yeshua so much that he had the courage to go ask the Roman governor, wicked Pontius Pilate, for the body of Jesus. One look at the face of our Lord, and we will understand why Joseph and Nicodemus were so particular with His body!

WOMEN WATCH THE BURIAL

Matthew 27:61
Mark 15:47
Luke 23:55–56

Do you remember the women who followed Jesus in Galilee? There was Joanna, the wife of Chuza, Herod's steward; Susanna; and Mary Magdalene, and others. They were there at the tomb, watching Joseph of Arimathea and Nicodemus as they laid the body of their Lord inside. It was not in Jewish manner for the women to mingle with the Sanhedrin.

Try to imagine how much love they had for Yeshua. They had walked behind Jesus and His disciples for months and months, and they had helped to finance the little band. Their lives had been changed by the power of the Messiah, and no doubt their hearts were pounding out of their chests as they saw what was being done to their Lord. True followers of the Messiah will never turn back!

The Sepulchre Sealed and Guarded

Matthew 27:62–66   To show how evil the chief priests and the Pharisees were, they went to Pilate on the Sabbath day and asked for the sepulchre to be sealed and guarded. They were afraid of the disciples stealing the body of Jesus, calling Jesus a "deceiver." Or, were they *really* afraid of what Jesus said would happen: "After three days I will rise again"!

THE RESURRECTION
OF THE MESSIAH

Matthew 28:1–10
Mark 16:1–11
Luke 24:1–12
John 20:1–18

It was prophesied in Psalm 16:10: "Neither wilt thou suffer thine Holy One to see corruption." It was believed in the time of Jesus that the soul hovered over the body until the third day, and after that there was no hope. The fourth day was when Lazarus's body began to stink (John 11:39). But the body of the Messiah would not stink, and would not see corruption. Jesus had told the disciples on many occasions that He would rise the *third day.*

Any part of a day or night was considered a whole day. So Jesus was crucified on Friday, was buried on Saturday, and He arose on Sunday. He was crucified on the Feast of Passover, buried on the Feast of Unleavened Bread, and He arose on the Feast of Firstfruits.

The saddest day the world has ever known was when "he cried with a loud voice, and yielded up the ghost." The most wonderful day the world has ever known was when the angel said, "He is not here: for he is risen."

One of the verses that touches me deeply is Mark 16:9: "Now when Jesus was risen early the first day of the week, he appeared *first* to Mary Magdalene, out of whom he had cast seven devils." Why did Jesus appear first to Mary Magdalene? Why not Peter, or John, or one of the disciples? Mary, in my opinion, understood more at this time than the disciples did, even though she was still afraid. When she came with the other women from Galilee and told the disciples what the angels had said, the disciples did not believe them (Luke 24:11).

She loved Jesus so much, and had experienced so much mercy from Jesus, that she had a greater amount of faith at this point. When we want to see Jesus more than anything or anyone, then He makes himself known to us!

The resurrection of the Messiah is the foundation of the Christian faith. If the Roman soldiers could have presented the dead body of Jesus, Christianity would have died in the first century. If the chief priests and Pharisees could have presented the dead body of Jesus, Christianity would have died in the first century. What has kept Christianity alive over the centuries is the fact, that a man called Jesus, Yeshua, died on a tree, and walked out of the tomb. It's not fiction, it is a historical fact! Without the risen Savior, there is *no hope* for anyone.

When Jesus raised Jairus' daughter, when He raised the widow's son at Nain, when He raised Lazarus, these were all *examples* of what was going to happen. Death could not hold the perfect Son of God! If Yeshua had not been God, then death would have won the victory.

Would God create the heavens and the earth, the sun, the moon, and the stars, and then make man and provide for him the things he needs in this life, and then, in a few years, be gone forever? All of creation would be in vain, if this life was the end for man. All of nature speaks out loudly that there is a Resurrection. Think of the fall, when leaves and flowers look so dead, and then think of the springtime, when the leaves come back out and the flowers bloom again. Are we so blind that we cannot see what God is trying to say to us?

There is an eternity for everyone. The lost will live forever, and so will the saved. The difference is, one will live forever in hell, and one will live forever in heaven. (I didn't write the Bible, God did!) What we choose to do with the Messiah will determine where we will spend eternity. Jesus said there will be "a resurrection of life," and "a resurrection of damnation" (John 5:29). But the point is, there *will be* a resurrection for everyone!

To prove how important the resurrection of the Messiah really is, the Scriptures tell us in 1 Corinthians 15, "If there be no resurrection . . . our preaching [is in] vain, and your faith is also vain. . . . Ye are yet in your sins. Then they also which are fallen asleep in Christ are perished. If in this life only we have hope in Christ, we are of all men most miserable" (1 Cor. 15:13–19).

My friends, when Mary Magdalene came to the tomb, very early in the morning on the first day of the week, she saw the stone rolled away. The stone was not rolled away to allow Jesus *to get out* of the tomb, but to allow her and the disciples *to see inside*. They *witnessed* what Jesus had told them back at Galilee: "The Son of Man must be delivered into the hands of sinful men, and be crucified, and the third day rise again" (Luke 24:7).

We live in a world of modern-day technology, and most people refuse to believe in the supernatural. Biblical Christianity is supernatural from the beginning to the end. It is humanly impossible for someone to die and rise again, but with God all things are possible. This brings us to the most important question. Who was Jesus of Nazareth? Who was Yeshua Ben Yoseph? He had to be none other than God in the flesh! No one could have ever fulfilled all those Hebrew Scriptures but Jesus of Nazareth. If Christianity is not something bigger than we are, then it would be useless for us to believe. Our hope is greater than our minds can conceive. Jesus is more wonderful than we could ever hope for. And just to think, He said, "I am the resurrection and the life: he that believeth in me, though he were dead, yet shall he live" (John 11:25).

King of Kings

Messiah came to earth,
Jesus was His name.
God became a man
To die for all our shame.
How He suffered, only heaven knows
But the third day He arose.

He is the King of kings and Lord of lords.
Jesus died and rose again.
He is the King of kings and Lord of lords,
His kingdom will never end.

He hung on the cross
For all the world to see.
He paid the sacrifice just for you and me.
His hands and feet were nailed
But righteousness prevailed.

He is the King of kings and Lord of lords.
Jesus died and rose again.
He is the King of kings and Lord of lords,
His kingdom will never end.

Written by Carroll Roberson. Copyright: Jesus Is Real Music (BMI)

ON THE ROAD TO EMMAUS

Luke 24:13–35 Almost all professing Christians have their favorite passages in the Bible. I have several, but this one holds a special place in my heart. In my personal study, there is a picture on the wall of the two men walking with Jesus on the road to Emmaus. I have had the wonderful opportunity to go to Emmaus, and I wish that everyone could experience walking on that old road, and reading this passage.

There are some rich lessons for us here, so let's not move too quickly. The name of the village was *Ammaus*. One of the men walking was named, Cleopas, *Klofah*, who was married to the sister of the mother Mary (John 19:25). It was the same day that Jesus had risen from the dead, and these two men had heard the testimony of the women, but they did not believe. So they were walking back to Emmaus, which was just a few miles from Jerusalem. In a supernatural way, Jesus started walking with them, but they did not realize who He was. Jesus asked them why they were so sad. Then Cleopas said, "Art thou only a stranger in Jerusalem, and hast not known the things which are come to pass there in these days? And he said unto them, *What things?*" Now that seems to be a strange question for Jesus to ask, doesn't it? Jesus came all the way from heaven, was born of a virgin girl, lived on earth for 33 years, died on a tree, went to the heart of the earth and came back, and now He says, *"What things?"*

Well, they began to describe the happenings to Jesus, how that they had hoped that Jesus of Nazareth was the One who would redeem Israel. But He was crucified, and certain women which were with our company went to the grave, but found not His body. Can you just try to imagine the sadness on their faces. But then Jesus said, "O fools, and slow of heart to believe all that the prophets have spoken; Ought not Christ to have suffered these things, and to enter into His glory?" Then Jesus preached the greatest sermon that was ever heard: "And beginning at Moses and all the prophets, he expounded unto them in all the scriptures the things concerning himself." What a sermon that must have been! In those days, they only had the Old Testament, the Hebrew Scriptures, and the Messiah Jesus went back and explained all the Scriptures that pertained to himself. No doubt, He told them about "the seed of the woman," "the seed of Abraham," the tribe of Judah," "the house of David," "a virgin shall conceive," "the town of Bethlehem," "the suffering servant," and all the Psalms. The greatest sermon that was ever given, was given to just two men.

When they drew nigh unto the village of Emmaus, Jesus "made as though he would have gone further." Jesus used this same mysterious technique when He walked on the water in Mark 6:48, and made

The Christ:

as though He would have passed by them. Jesus had no intention of passing the disciples by that night on the sea, and He had no intention of passing by the home of the two men at Emmaus. This seems so strange. However, Jesus seems to do strange things at times, in order to get us to call out to Him. The disciples cried out to Him from the boat on the Sea of Galilee. Here, the two men constrain Him to come inside. It was getting late in the evening, so they had a meal together, like Jesus was always doing with His followers. "When Jesus broke the bread, and blessed it, and gave it to them, their eyes were opened, and they knew Him." Maybe it was the way He broke the bread, maybe it was the blessing He spoke, or maybe it was the way He handed the bread to them. Some have said that maybe they saw the nail prints in His hands. Whatever it was, they recognized that this stranger was Jesus of Nazareth, and *He was alive!*

Jesus vanished out of their sight, and they said one to another, "Did not our heart burn within us, while He talked with us by the way, and while He opened to us the Scriptures?" They had *sad hearts* when Jesus starting walking with them, they had *doubtful hearts* when they told Jesus about what had happened in Jerusalem, but now they had *burning hearts*, and they ran back to Jerusalem with *satisfied hearts.*

There have been times in my Christian life when the Lord seemed far away, but those times were there so I would learn to call out to Him. In my life I have been sad and I have been doubtful, but since I met Jesus, my heart has been set on fire, and I have found true satisfaction in serving Yeshua, the Messiah! I can't help but do what these two men on the road to Emmaus did — they went quickly, and told the other disciples that the Lord is risen indeed!

BLESSED ARE THEY
THAT HAVE NOT SEEN

John 20:24–31   Jesus had appeared to the disciples on the same day of the Resurrection, but Thomas was not there. Eight days later, Thomas was with the disciples, as they were gathered behind closed doors. "Then came Jesus, the doors being shut, and stood in the midst, and said, peace be unto you. Then saith he to Thomas, Reach hither thy finger, and behold my hands; and reach hither thy hand, and thrust it into my side; and be not faithless, but believing. And Thomas answered and said unto him, My Lord and my God. Jesus saith unto him, Thomas, because thou hast seen me, thou hast believed; blessed are they that have *not* seen, and yet have believed."

Thomas has been criticized over the years, and called "the doubting Thomas." But really, all of the disciples doubted until they saw Jesus. Jesus knew that Thomas loved Him, and He made a special appearance while Thomas was there. The Lord showed such compassion to His disciples, even when they were not everything they were supposed to be. The statement that Thomas made shows the deity of Jesus: "My Lord and my God." Jesus is Lord, and He is God! Thomas believed because He saw the Lord, but Jesus gave a special blessing to all of us who have never seen Him with our natural eyes. We are "blessed," Jesus said, if we believe in Him and have not seen Him. I'm reminded of what Peter said in 1 Peter 1:8, "Whom having not seen, ye love." We haven't seen Jesus yet, but we know Him by faith, and we love Him!

John closes this chapter with a powerful statement: "And many other signs truly did Jesus in the presence of his disciples, which are not written in this book; But these are written, that ye might believe that Jesus is the Christ (Messiah), the Son of God; and that believing ye might have life through his name." The apostle John is saying that there were other things that Jesus did which were written in the other Gospel accounts, but also he was saying that not all of the things Jesus did were written down. The Holy Spirit brought to the disciples minds what to write down. The things that were written, the miracles, the parables, the Crucifixion, the Resurrection, were recorded so that people would believe that Jesus is the Messiah! When a person believes in Jesus as the Messiah, they receive life, and life eternal!

MEET ME BACK AT GALILEE

John 21 Jesus had told the disciples back in the Garden of Gethsemane, "But after I am risen again, I will go before you into Galilee" (Matt. 26:32). The angels told the women at the garden tomb, "And, behold, he goeth before you into Galilee; there shall ye see him" (Matt. 28:7). Then when Jesus met the women as they were going to tell the disciples that Jesus had risen, Jesus told them, "Go tell my brethren that they go into Galilee, and there shall they see me" (Matt. 28:10).

So there is something very special about this place called Galilee. Why? This is where the Messiah lived and started His ministry. This is where most of the miracles were performed. This is where He first called the disciples to follow Him. There is something different about seeing the Lord in a religious city like Jerusalem, and then seeing Him back in the common, everyday settings of Galilee. We can boast about what a good service we had at church on Sunday, but experiencing God in our everyday lives is totally different. So Jesus calls them to go back to Galilee, there they will *see Him!*

This brings us to this unique, and powerful chapter in John's Gospel. We shall divide this chapter into three sections.

1) OUR LIVES MUST BE DIRECTED BY THE MESSIAH

John 21:3–14: Peter decides to go fishing, and the other disciples follow him. They fish all night, and catch nothing. When the morning came, Jesus stood on the shore and told them to cast their nets on

The Christ:

the right side of the ship. They caught such a multitude of fishes, that it took all of the other disciples to pull in the net. When they came to the shore, Jesus already had a fire built, and fish and bread for them to eat.

The lesson is, when the disciples followed their own leadership, they caught nothing, but when they did what Jesus said, they caught a multitude. As long we live our lives *directed* by our own selfish desires, we will be of no service in God's kingdom. It is only when our lives are *directed* by the Messiah Jesus that we become useful. This was also a completion of the miracle in Luke 5. Then, the fish net broke, but here it did *not* break. Why? Because before, the Messiah had not been crucified and risen, but here, Jesus had died on the cross, and was alive again. It was going to take the death, burial, and resurrection of the Messiah, before the disciples could *really* be fishers of men.

2) OUR LIVES MUST BE MOTIVATED BY OUR LOVE FOR THE MESSIAH

John 21:15–17: Jesus was always eating with His disciples, because it was a symbol of forgiveness and reconciliation. Here, He is showing His great love for them, and preparing them for their future mission. Try to imagine how Peter must be feeling at this time. He cursed and denied the Lord three times back in Jerusalem, as he warmed himself by a fire. Here, the Lord has another fire prepared for him. What is the Lord going to say? Is He going to throw Peter away for his terrible mistake?

Jesus saith to Simon Peter, "Lovest thou me more than these?" Three times Peter had denied Christ, here Jesus asks Peter three times, "Lovest thou me?" Did Peter love Jesus more than the other disciples? Did Peter love Jesus more than the fishing boats? Peter said something very interesting in verse 17, "Lord, thou knowest all things; thou knowest that I love thee." In spite of Peter's failures, Jesus *knew* that Peter loved Him. Peter had a lot to learn about serving the Master, but he did love Him!

Sometimes we are like Peter, in that we fail the Lord, too, but He knows that we still love Him. When our lives are motivated by love for the Messiah, we may fall, but we get up and keep on keeping on. We must love Jesus more than anything, or anybody in this life. More than our families, more than our church, even more than we love ourselves.

3) WE MUST BE FAITHFUL UNTO DEATH

John 21:18–23: Jesus began to tell Peter that one day he would die for Him. Then He said to Peter, "Follow me." Peter was worried about John, and he wanted to know what was going to happen to John. Jesus told Peter, "If I will that he tarry till I come, what is that to thee? Follow thou me." Peter could not follow the Messiah faithfully as long as he was worried about how John was going to die.

We must keep our minds and hearts on what God has for us to do in this life, and be faithful unto death. If we live a short while, or if we live to be old, is not the important matter. It's what we do with what we've got. We get into spiritual trouble when we become jealous of God's servants. If we are faithful in what He has given us to do, then we won't have time to meddle in other people's business. Life is short — we must make it count!

I Love Jesus

I love Jesus more today,
More today than yesterday.
I love Jesus more today
But not as much as tomorrow,
Not as much as tomorrow.

When I denied my Lord
He didn't throw me away.
Even though I failed Him
to the Cross He took my place.

I love Jesus more today,
More today than yesterday.
I love Jesus more today
But not as much as tomorrow,
Not as much as tomorrow.

In Messiah's kingdom
Could I ever find a place?
He has so much mercy
All my sins He erased.

Written by Carroll Roberson. Copyright: Jesus Is Real Music (BMI)

THE GREAT COMMISSION

Matthew 28:16–20
Mark 16:14–18

Important events seem to happen on mountains in the Bible. The Great Commission is certainly an important event. Jesus had appointed a certain mountain where they were to meet Him. Maybe it was where the Sermon on the Mount was given. Maybe it was on top of Mount Arbel, that overlooks the entire Sea of Galilee. We do not know where, but we do know what He told them.

The disciples still had some doubts, (verse 17), but they worshiped Jesus when they saw Him. Jesus told them, "All power is given unto me in heaven and in earth." Jesus the Messiah was the judge over all mankind, and had the power to give eternal life to all who believed in Him.

"Go ye therefore, and teach all nations, baptizing them in the name of the Father, and the Son, and of the Holy Ghost: Teaching them to observe all things whatsoever I have commanded you: and lo, I am with you always, even unto the end of the world. Amen."

Twice in this passage, Jesus uses the words "teach" or "teaching." This passage has been used throughout the centuries as a command of Jesus to evangelize the world. That may be true, but the main truth, is to make disciples. "Teach all nations." Not only were they to preach the gospel, but they were to teach the nations and baptize the believers. Water baptism was a means of being identified with the Messiah. As the New Testament progresses, the real baptism is the baptism of the Holy Spirit (Rom. 6:3–4 and 1 Cor. 12:13). Many Hebrew scholars believe that Jesus was referring to the Holy Spirit in this passage. Notice the word "name" is singular, but Jesus mentions three names, "the Father, the Son, and the Holy Ghost." God is *one,* but there are three persons in the Trinity.

After a person is saved, they must be taught the Holy Scriptures. The number one problem in churches today is biblical illiteracy. People have not been properly taught the Scriptures over the years, and this leads to many people not being saved, and many saved people being carnal.

Jesus gives them the promise that He will always be with them. When the Messiah came into the world, His name was "Emmanuel, which being interpreted is, *God with us*." (Matt. 1:23). At the close of His earthly ministry, Jesus assures them that He will be with them forever.

In Mark's account, we find that the believers in Messiah will "cast out devils, and speak with new tongues. They shall take up serpents: and if they drink any deadly thing, it shall not hurt them; and they shall lay hands on the sick, and they shall recover." These verses have caused a tremendous amount of controversy over the centuries. But when they are taken in the proper context, they can be easily understood. When the disciples started taking the message of Jesus being the Messiah into Israel and the rest of the world, they would have certain supernatural gifts, to prove they had been with Jesus. We see these gifts in the Book of Acts, as new languages were given to certain people in order to communicate the gospel. The word "tongues," *glossa*, means "a language not learned." Many of the new believers would speak in a language they had never been taught. In the Middle East, it is very common for people to speak more than one language, so there was a great need for the gift of "tongues" or "languages" to be used.

The apostle Paul was bitten by a viper in Acts 28:3, but it did not harm him. He was taking the gospel to the Gentiles, and God protected Him from serpents. If the followers of Jesus were forced to drink a deadly drink, it would not kill them until God's mission was accomplished. These verses do not mean that we are to handle snakes, or drink poison today, just tempting the Lord. If God has a work for us to do, He certainly will protect us until that job is completed.

Physical healing was seen in the Book of Acts, but as we go through the New Testament, it seems to diminish somewhat (Phil. 2:26; 2 Tim. 4:20). God still heals people today, but it does not have the same purpose as it did in the first century. I have been healed by the hand of God on many occasions, but we should not exalt physical healing above spiritual salvation.

There are many gifts of the Spirit, but the greatest gift is *love!* We must rightly divide the Word of truth, lest we fall into error. When we get our focus off of Jesus, we have lost the purpose of the Holy Spirit. He is to point people to the Messiah! "He shall glorify me" (John 16:14).

THE ASCENSION
OF THE MESSIAH

Mark 16:19
Luke 24:50–51
Acts 1:6–11

When the Messiah came into this world, He entered through a poor village called Bethlehem. When He was about to leave this world, He once again went to a poor village, called Bethany. Bethany was on the eastern slope of the Mount of Olives, where Jesus had been received several times by His closest friends. Here, He takes the disciples, and He lifts up those precious nail-scarred hands, and blesses them. "While he blessed them, he was parted from them, and carried up into heaven." During the blessing, the disciples were blessed to see their Master ascend up into heaven. Part of that blessing is found in Acts 1:8, "But ye shall receive power, after that the Holy Ghost is come upon you; and ye shall be witnesses unto me both in Jerusalem, and in all Judaea, and in Samaria, and unto the uttermost part of the earth." He was assuring His disciples, that they *would* take His message into all the world.

"And when he had spoken these things, while they beheld, he was taken up; and a cloud received him out of their sight. And while they looked stedfastly toward heaven as he went up, behold, two men stood by them in white apparel; Which also said, Ye men of Galilee, why stand ye gazing up into heaven? This same Jesus, which is taken up from you into heaven, shall so come in like manner as ye have seen him go into heaven" (Acts 1:9–11). What a homecoming it must have been, when the Son of God went back to the Father. Jesus had told the disciples in John 16:28, "I came forth from the Father, and am come into the world; again, I leave the world, and go to the Father."

Angels were there when Jesus was born, angels were there when He was resurrected, and when He ascended into heaven. Jesus ascended in a cloud; He will return to earth in a cloud (Luke 21:27). The angels wanted the disciples to know that the very *same* Jesus would come back to earth one day. There's not two or three Messiahs, there's only one Messiah!

PROPHET, PRIEST, AND KING

Hebrews 1:1–3 — God, who at sundry times and in divers manners spake in time past unto the fathers by the prophets, hath in these last days spoken unto us by his Son, whom he hath appointed heir of all things, by whom also he made the worlds; Who being the brightness of his glory, and the express image of his person, and upholding all things by the word of his power, when he had by himself purged our sins, sat down on the right hand of the Majesty on high."

1) *Prophet:* The Messiah was certainly "the Prophet" that God promised would come into the world in Deuteronomy 18:15. Peter used this verse when preaching to the crowds in Acts 3:22. Think of all the great prophets of the Old Testament, like Isaiah, Elijah, Elisha, Jeremiah, Ezekiel, Daniel, Amos, Zechariah, Malachi, John the Baptist, and others. God spoke to His people through these prophets, *but now* God has spoken through His Son, the Messiah! Do you recall what God said out of the cloud, on the Mount of Transfiguration? "This is my beloved Son, in whom I am well pleased, *hear ye him.*" We are to listen to Jesus now. His words are the words of God. When we read the words written in red in the Gospels, they are the words of God, spoken through Jesus the Messiah! Jesus was the fulfillment of the *prophets*, for He was the *Prophet*.

2) *Priest:* Notice what the writer of the Book of Hebrews says: "When he had by himself purged our sins, sat down on the right hand of the Majesty on high." Under the old Jewish law, there was only one person who could enter the Holy of Holies, and

that was the high priest. And he could only enter once a year, on the Day of Atonement, to offer a sacrifice for the sins of the people. In the temple, which would have been equivalent to a billion-dollar building today, there were *no* chairs, because the high priest was not allowed to sit down. The true work of forgiveness of sins could not be completed until the Messiah came and died on the Cross. There were many high priests under the old Jewish law, but Jesus became the Great High Priest! By himself, He purged our sins, and is now seated at the right hand of God. We, as believers need to understand the *present* work of the Messiah. He is interceding for His children in heaven today. He is our advocate. He is pleading our case to the Heavenly Father. When we fall short and sin, as believers, Jesus is going to the Father on our behalf. But as far as our sins are concerned, all of our mistakes have been paid for and the work has been done: *"It is finished!"* It's not God doing His part, and we doing ours. It's not by grace *and* works — it is all by God's eternal grace that anyone is saved. This is what gets so many people into spiritual trouble. They try to add a good deed or a church ritual onto what the Messiah has done. True faith produces obedience, but salvation is of God, and God alone! Not only did the Messiah die, He arose. God accepted the payment that Jesus made for our sins.

3) *King:* Jesus the Messiah "made the worlds, and upholds everything by the word of His power." Herod the Great thought he was the king when Jesus was born, but Jesus was the true King! Herod Antipas, who lived in Galilee, thought he was the king, but little did he know that the man they called Jesus, who was walking on the shores, was the true King of the universe. Pontius Pilate thought he was the ruler when Jesus was crucified, but little did he know, that the one he crucified was the King of glory! Have you ever wondered why Jesus *accepted* worship from His followers? He was the King when He was born, and He was the King when He died. He has been appointed heir of all things. One day, He will return to earth, and "he shall shew, who is the blessed and only Potentate, the King of kings, and Lord of lords" (1 Tim. 6:15).

The Christ:

THE UNIQUE
MESSIAH

His birth was contrary to the laws of life. His death was contrary to the laws of death. He had no cornfields or fisheries, but He could spread a table for five thousand and have bread and fish to spare. He walked on no beautiful carpets or velvet rugs, but He walked on the waters of the Sea of Galilee.

When He died, few men mourned, but the sun was black at noon day. Though men trembled not for their sins, the earth beneath them shook. All nature honored Him. All of the animals worshiped Him. Sinners alone rejected Him.

Three years He preached His gospel. He wrote no book, built no church house, had no bank account. But after nineteen hundred years, He is the one central figure of human history.

He's unparalleled, He's unprecedented, He's indescribable, He's invincible, He's incomprehensible. He's the King of the Jews, He's the King of Israel, He's the King of righteousness, He's the King of the ages, He's the King of heaven, He's the King of glory, He's the King of kings and Lord of lords. There's only one MESSIAH! CHRIST — Jesus of Nazareth, I wonder if you know Him today?

There's Only One Messiah

The seed of a woman, the seed of Abraham
Through the tribe of Judah
Would come the great I Am.
In the house of David, a great king would rise
Be born of a virgin
Then be crucified.

There's only one Messiah,
Jesus is His name.
He died and rose again
The first time when He came.
Messiah will return,
His kingdom will come,
And Israel will know
That He is the promised one.

The blind would see, the lame would walk,
Demons cast out,
The deaf and dumb would talk.
No one had ever seen, anyone so kind,
Even the little children
Saw the love in his eyes.

There's only one Messiah,
Jesus is His name.
He died and rose again
The first time when He came.
Messiah will return,
His kingdom will come,
And Israel will know
That He is the promised one.

THE CITY OF JERUSALEM

Over the centuries, Jerusalem has been called by many names: Salem, Jebus, the City of Peace, the City of David, the City of God, Zion, and, in Hebrew it is called *Yerushaliim*, and ends with a plural form of the Hebrew word for peace, *shalom*.

The name Jerusalem occurs over eight hundred times in the Bible, 667 times in the Old Testament, and 144 times in the New Testament.

Jerusalem today is a patchwork of buildings from different historical periods and also a patchwork of different people, both residents and visitors alike. You can find Christian pilgrims visiting from all over the world, to Hassidic Jews in their black tunics and side curls, to the Bedouins, who still live a primitive life on the hillsides.

In the time of Jesus, the population of Jerusalem would swell to about 250,000 people during the biblical feasts each year. The Bible says in Zechariah 14:16 that when the Messiah returns, all nations of the earth will come up to Jerusalem each year and celebrate the Feast of Tabernacles.

Today there are nine gates, entering into the walls of the city: the New Gate, the Damascus Gate, Herod's Gate, the Lion's Gate (St. Stephen's Gate), the Eastern or Golden Gate, the Dung Gate, Zion's Gate, the Tanner's Gate, and Jaffa Gate. From the gates of Jerusalem, the prophets thundered, and just outside the northern gate is where the Messiah was crucified and rose again.

In the Old Testament, Jerusalem was the spiritual and administrative capital of Israel. From here, the king ruled, and God's presence was in the temple. During the time of Jesus there was not a king ruling, because the true King had come, *Yeshua ha Mashiach*. The Messiah is coming back to Jerusalem, where He will establish the millennial kingdom for a thousand years. He will rule and reign from Jerusalem.

However, today, religious Jews pray at a small section of an outer retaining wall of the Temple Mount that was built by Herod the Great, known as the Western Wall. One day there will be a third temple built, where the Messiah will rule and reign as King. How and when this happen, only God knows.

Because this is God's city, it has been fought over by more nations than any city on earth. What a paradox that Jerusalem is known as the "city of peace," but has undergone 37 conquests, and has changed hands 86 times.

There were no main trade routes here, no major waterways; it was the place of worship that made it the center of Israel. God is what drew people to this city, and it has remained the center of the world, even today.

The Christ:

Jesus wept over this city, and prophesied a day when Israel would recognize Him as their Messiah (Matt. 23:37–39). He also said that "Jerusalem shall be trodden down of the Gentiles, until the times of the Gentiles be fulfilled" (Luke 21:24). From the time of Nebuchadnezzar, the king of Babylon, Jerusalem was in the hands of the Gentiles, other than a few years (165 B.C.–63 B.C., the Hasmonean dynasty). No king from the tribe of Judah, from the house of David, has reigned in Jerusalem in over 2,500 years. This prophecy must be fulfilled (1 Chron. 17:11–14; Luke 1:32–33).

I find it amazing that we are living in the time when God is restoring Israel, and preparing them for the coming of the King of kings. Never in the history of the world has a nation been exiled for almost 1,900 years and then has risen up again to become a nation. From the time of Hadrian, the Roman emperor, in A.D. 135, when Jerusalem was renamed *Aelia Capitalina*, until 1948, Israel was not a nation. The Jews were scattered into all the world. In Ezekiel 37, God said the dry bones would live again. There are approximately six million Jews in the land today. The Jordan valley, which just a few years ago was barren and desolate, is now blossoming like a rose, exporting over five million flowers a day. The Jordan valley now produces some of the sweetest fruit in the world. Land that once was only an infested marsh in the Huleh Valley, in northern Galilee, is now rich, fertile, farm fields.

The Lord said in Jeremiah 16:14–15 that there will come a day when He will do a greater miracle than bringing the children of Israel out of Egypt, He will bring them back to the land of Israel, and we are seeing that happen today.

God has called us into an ongoing redemption process that is strongly connected to the land of Israel. God is not only preparing this land for the second coming of the Messiah, but He is preparing a people as well. We are called to be a watchman over the city of Jerusalem and the Jewish nation. This is why I believe America has been so richly blessed, because they have supported Israel over the years (Gen.12:3).

There is a revival going on in many Christian circles today, going back to the Jewish roots of the Christian faith. Many are realizing that

Christianity did not begin in Rome, or Greece, or England, or not even in the United States, but in Israel.

Christianity is strongly connected to Jerusalem. From this city of Jerusalem, the Messiah was crucified, buried, and rose again. He ascended from the Mount of Olives, the Holy Spirit came down on the Day of Pentecost here, and the first church council was in Jerusalem. This is where the Messiah will return, and plant His feet on the Mount of Olives (Zech. 14:4).

And the Lord shall be king over all the earth (Zech. 14:9).

And blessed be his glorious name for ever: and let the whole earth be filled with his glory; Amen, and Amen (Ps. 72:19).

FINAL THOUGHTS

God has blessed the entire world with salvation through the Messiah, who came to us as a descendant of Abraham, Isaac, and Jacob, the root of Jesse, and the house of David. The Jewish people are still alive, and they are now coming back to the land of Israel by the thousands. Deuteronomy 30:1–5 tells us that God will bring them back to the land, and God will gather them from all the nations of the earth. In Jeremiah 31:35–36, the Scriptures tell us that as long as the sun shines by day, and the moon and stars by night, there will be a nation called Israel. Zechariah 2:8 calls Israel the "apple of God's eye." Zechariah 9:16 says that one day Israel will shine like "jewels in a crown."

The believing Gentiles have not only received salvation, but they have become partakers of the covenant promises that God gave to Israel. This does not mean that the Church has taken the place of Israel. God will deal with Israel in the very near future again. We are in debt to the Jewish people. They gave us the Bible, and they gave us the Messiah. The gospel is to the Jew first, then to the Greek (Rom. 1:16).

The stage is being set for the second coming of the Messiah. We are called to be a part of this prophecy. As we support Israel, and pray for the peace of Jerusalem, we are praying for the Prince of Peace to come. Our job is to be faithful in spreading the gospel of Yeshua throughout the world.

If you are an unbelieving Jew, I challenge you to search the Old Testament passages like Isaiah 53, Psalm 22, and hundreds of others. Then read the four Gospel accounts of Matthew, Mark, Luke, and

John. You will see that there is only one person who could have possibly fulfilled those prophecies — Jesus of Nazareth!

If you are an unbelieving Gentile, how grateful you should be that God, in His mercy and grace, has extended a call to you. We are living in the "times of the Gentiles" now, when *we* can become part of God's family. That door is swiftly closing, when God will turn back to the nation of Israel (Rom. 11:25).

Please receive Jesus the Messiah, as your personal Savior, before it is too late. Whether you be Jew or Gentile, the message is, *"Ashrey hakoreh beShem Adonay,"* "Blessed is he who calls on the name of the Lord."

SUGGESTED READING

Edersheim, Alfred. *The Life and Times of Jesus the Messiah*. Peabody, MA: Hendrickson, 1993.

Fruchtenbaum, Arnold. Various website articles at Ariel Ministries, <www.ariel.org>.

Green, J.P., Sr. *The Interlinear Bible*. Peabody, MA: Hendrickson, 1986).

Howard, Kevin, and Marvin Rosenthal, *The Feasts of the Lord*. Orlando, FL: Zion's Hope; Nashville, TN: Nelson Pub., 1997.

Lascelle, Ruth Specter. *Pictures of the Messiah*. Arlington, WA: Bedrock Publ., 1997.

Levitt, Zola. Various website articles at Zola Levitt Ministries, <www.levitt.com>.

McDowell, Josh. *Evidence That Demands a Verdict*. Nashville, TN: T. Nelson, 1993.

Pixner, Bargil. *With Jesus Through Galilee According to the Fifth Gospel*. Collegeville, MN: Liturgical Press, 1996.

Stern, David, translator. *Complete Jewish Bible*. Clarksville, MD: Jewish New Testament Publications, 1998.

Strong, James, LL.D., S.T.D. *The New Strong's Exhaustive Concordance of the Bible*. Nashville, TN: T. Nelson, 2001.

Zodhiates, Spiros, editor. *The Hebrew-Greek Key Study Bible*. Chattanooga, TN: AMG Pub., 1996.

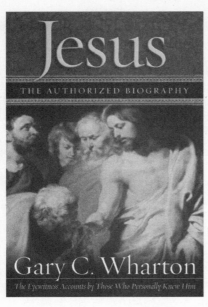

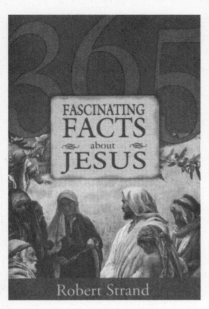

365 Fascinating Facts about Jesus

by Robert Strand

The political, cultural, and religious times in which Jesus lived are brought to life in this terrific book. Fact by fact, the history of His birth, life, death, and resurrection are recounted along with the rich traditions and customs of His people. The interesting information also includes fascinating articles about many things related to Christ, such as the wise men who visited Him after His birth, Da Vinci's Last Supper, the Via Dolorosa, the calendar, the Wailing Wall, and much more.

ISBN-13: 978-0-89221-488-4
ISBN-10: 0-89221-488-0
224 pages • paperback • $10.99

SONG TITLES FROM THE CD

1. Walk This Land with Me
   by Carroll Roberson

2. There's Only One Messiah
   by Carroll Roberson

3. His Name Shall Be Called Wonderful
   by Carroll Roberson

4. Down to the Jordan
   by Carroll Roberson

5. Galilee, Galilee
   by Carroll Roberson

6. Cast Your Net upon the Sea
   by Carroll Roberson

7. Bread of Life
   by Carroll Roberson and Nathan Wood

8. I Love Jesus
   by Carroll Roberson

9. 23rd Psalm
   by Dan Jividen

10. A Time to Live
    by Carroll Roberson

11. King of Kings
    by Carroll Roberson

12. The Love of God
    by Carroll Roberson

13. Fill My Cup
    by Carroll Roberson

14. Let Me Touch Him
    by Carroll Roberson

15. Such Is the Kingdom of Heaven
    by Carroll Roberson

16. Jesus Is the Master
    by Carroll Roberson

17. Yeshua Is Messiah
    by Carroll Roberson